UNCOMMON MEASURES
Equivalence and Linkage Among Educational Tests

Michael J. Feuer, Paul W. Holland, Bert F. Green,
Meryl W. Bertenthal, and F. Cadelle Hemphill, *Editors*

Committee on Equivalency and Linkage of Educational Tests

Board on Testing and Assessment

Commission on Behavioral and Social Sciences and Education

National Research Council

NATIONAL ACADEMY PRESS
Washington, D.C. 1999

NATIONAL ACADEMY PRESS   2101 Constitution Avenue, N.W.   Washington, D.C. 20418

NOTICE: The project that is the subject of this report was approved by the Governing Board of the National Research Council, whose members are drawn from the councils of the National Academy of Sciences, the National Academy of Engineering, and the Institute of Medicine. The members of the committee responsible for the report were chosen for their special competences and with regard for appropriate balance.

The study was supported by Contract/Grant No. ED-98-CO-0005 between the National Academy of Sciences and the U.S. Department of Education. Any opinions, findings, conclusions, or recommendations expressed in this publication are those of the author(s) and do not necessarily reflect the view of the organizations or agencies that provided support for this project.

Library of Congress Cataloging-in-Publication Data

Uncommon measures : equivalence and linkage among educational tests
/ Michael J. Feuer, ... [et al.], editors ; Committee on
Equivalency and Linkage of Educational Tests.
    p. cm.
    Includes bibliographical references.
    ISBN 0-309-06279-9
    1. Educational tests and measurements—United
States—Interpretation. 2. National Assessment of Educational
Progress (Project) I. Feuer, Michael J. II. National Research
Council (U.S.). Committee on Equivalency and Linkage of Educational
Tests.
    LB3060.8 .U53 1999
    371.26'0973—dc21   98-40263

Additional copies of this report are available from National Academy Press, 2101 Constitution Avenue, N.W., Washington, D.C. 20418

Call (800) 624-6242 or (202) 334-3313 (in the Washington metropolitan area)

This report is also available online at **http://www.nap.edu**

Printed in the United States of America

COMMITTEE ON EQUIVALENCY AND LINKAGE OF EDUCATIONAL TESTS

BOARD ON TESTING AND ASSESSMENT

Foreword

President Clinton's 1997 proposal to create voluntary national tests in reading and mathematics catapulted testing to the top of the national education agenda. The proposal turned up the volume on what had already been a contentious debate and drew intense scrutiny from a wide range of educators, parents, policy makers, and social scientists. Recognizing the important role science could play in sorting through the passionate and often heated exchanges in the testing debate, Congress and the Clinton administration asked the National Research Council, through its Board on Testing and Assessment (BOTA), to conduct three fast-track studies over a 10-month period.

This report and its companions—*Evaluation of the Voluntary National Tests: Phase 1* and *High Stakes: Testing for Tracking, Promotion, and Graduation*—are the result of truly heroic efforts on the part of the BOTA members, the study committee chairs and members, two co-principal investigators, consultants, and staff, who all understood the urgency of the mission and rose to the challenge of a unique and daunting timeline. Michael Feuer, BOTA director, deserves the special thanks of the board for keeping the effort on track and shepherding the report through the review process. His dedicated effort, long hours, sage advice, and good humor were essential to the success of this effort. Paul Holland, a member of the Board, deserves our deepest appreciation for his superb leadership of the committee that produced this report.

These reports are exemplars of the Research Council's commitment to scientific rigor in the public interest: they provide clear and compelling statements of the underlying issues, cogent answers to nettling questions, and highly readable findings and recommendations. These reports will help illuminate the toughest issues in the ongoing debate over the proposed Voluntary National Tests. But they will do much more as well. The issues addressed in this and the other two reports go well beyond the immediate national testing proposal: they have much to contribute to knowledge about the way tests—all tests—are planned, designed, implemented, reported, and used for a variety of education policy goals.

I know the whole board joins me in expressing our deepest gratitude to the many people who worked so hard on this project. These reports will advance the debate over the role of testing in American education, and I am honored to have participated in this effort.

Robert L. Linn, *Chair*
Board on Testing and Assessment

Acknowledgments

This project would not have been feasible without the extraordinary contributions of many individuals and without the generosity of many institutions.

We acknowledge with deep gratitude the indefatigable Bob Linn, who, as chair of the Board on Testing and Assessment (BOTA), again supplied wise counsel at every stage of the committee's work. Carl Kaestle, vice chair of BOTA, graciously helped us straighten out our understanding of the historical context of standards-based reform and the federal role in education. Other BOTA members also participated in numerous briefings, read earlier drafts, and made invaluable suggestions for improved language and tone.

We thank our exemplary staff: Meryl Bertenthal, Cadelle Hemphill, and Lisa Alston, who joined the BOTA team only 9 months ago and quickly mastered the many aspects of their new jobs. Having now successfully completed the equivalent of a marathon-length run at the pace of a half-mile sprint, they are poised for continued involvement in many of BOTA's future projects.

We have been most fortunate to work with Bert Green, an outstanding statistician whose wisdom and scholarship is reflected throughout the report. Bert attended all the meetings, worked tirelessly for greater precision in our language, and was a wonderful colleague.

Other members of the BOTA staff—Bob Rothman, Karen Mitchell, Patricia Morison, Viola Horek, Naomi Chudowsky, Lee Jones, Kim

Saldin, Alix Beatty, Allison Black, and Steve Baldwin offered advice and support and worked again as an invaluable team even though busy with their respective projects. Nancy Kober's fine editorial and substantive judgment is again evident in this report, for which we thank her.

Barbara Torrey, executive director of the Commission on Behavioral and Social Sciences and Education (CBASSE), and Sandy Wigdor, director of CBASSE's Division on Education, Labor, and Human Performance, have been sources of great encouragement and paved many paths from committee formation through report review. We are indebted, also, to the whole CBASSE staff for indulging our scheduling exigencies. Thanks also to Sally Stanfield and the whole Audubon team at the National Academy Press, for their creative and speedy support.

Extra special thanks to Eugenia Grohman, the CBASSE associate director of reports. It is hard to imagine how we could have accomplished this and our other concurrent studies without Genie's expert judgment and finely tuned skill at editing and navigating multiple manuscripts. Only grudgingly do we accept that she will now have to turn more of her attention to other CBASSE projects.

A word of acknowledgment to the sponsors of this study. We have benefited from supportive and collegial relations with members of the various House and Senate committee staffs—on both sides of the aisle—for whom the results of our work have such important implications. We thank them all for understanding and respecting the process of the National Research Council (NRC). Our contracting officer's technical representative, Holly Spurlock, of the U.S. Department of Education, has been a most effective project officer; we thank her for her patience and guidance throughout. Many other officials in the department, the National Assessment Governing Board, and in numerous private and public organizations involved in testing also deserve our thanks and recognition for their cooperation in providing information. The following individuals provided materials or made presentations to the committee: Edward Slawski, Harcourt Brace Educational Measurement; Sarah Hennings, Riverside Publishing; Stephanie Gertz, CTB/McGraw Hill; Wayne Martin, Council of Chief State School Officers; Bob Schwartz and Matt Gandal, Achieve, Inc.; Don McLaughlin, American Institutes for Research; Mark Wilson, University of California at Berkeley, and Wendy Yen, CTB/McGraw Hill. Their contributions were helpful to the committee's deliberations.

This report has been reviewed by individuals chosen for their diverse perspectives and technical expertise, in accordance with procedures approved by the NRC's Report Review Committee. The purpose of this independent review is to provide candid and critical comments that will assist the authors and the NRC in making the published report as sound as possible and to ensure that the report meets institutional standards for objectivity, evidence, and responsiveness to the study charge. The content of the review comments and draft manuscript remain confidential to protect the integrity of the deliberative process.

We thank the following individuals, who are neither officials nor employees of the NRC, for their participation in the review of this report: Robert Brennan, College of Education, University of Iowa; Arthur S. Goldberger, Department of Economics, University of Wisconsin; Lyle V. Jones, L.L. Thurstone Psychometric Laboratory, University of North Carolina, Chapel Hill; Lincoln E. Moses, Department of Statistics (professor emeritus), Stanford University; Stephen W. Raudenbush, School of Education, University of Michigan; Henry W. Riecken, Professor of Behavioral Sciences (emeritus), University of Pennsylvania School of Medicine; Richard Shavelson, School of Education, Stanford University; Mark Wilson, School of Education, University of California, Berkeley.

Although the individuals listed above provided many constructive comments and suggestions, responsibility for the final content of this report rests solely with the authoring committee and the NRC.

Above all, we thank the members of the committee, who understood both the urgency and significance of their charge, gave generously of their expertise and time, and met the highest standards of the 130-year old tradition of the National Academy complex in providing voluntary scientific advice to the government. That so many of them were willing and able to add hours to their already full days, and to share their wisdom with grace, humor, and impeccable rigor, is evidence of their commitment to scholarship in the public interest.

Finally, we thank Roberta Holland for her patience, understanding, and good humor during our work on this project. No more 7 a.m. phone calls!

Paul W. Holland, *Chair*
Michael J. Feuer, *Study Director*
Committee on Equivalency and Linkage
of Educational Tests

The National Academy of Sciences is a private, nonprofit, self-perpetuating society of distinguished scholars engaged in scientific and engineering research, dedicated to the furtherance of science and technology and to their use for the general welfare. Upon the authority of the charter granted to it by the Congress in 1863, the Academy has a mandate that requires it to advise the federal government on scientific and technical matters. Dr. Bruce M. Alberts is president of the National Academy of Sciences.

The National Academy of Engineering was established in 1964, under the charter of the National Academy of Sciences, as a parallel organization of outstanding engineers. It is autonomous in its administration and in the selection of its members, sharing with the National Academy of Sciences the responsibility for advising the federal government. The National Academy of Engineering also sponsors engineering programs aimed at meeting national needs, encourages education and research, and recognizes the superior achievements of engineers. Dr. William A. Wulf is president of the National Academy of Engineering.

The Institute of Medicine was established in 1970 by the National Academy of Sciences to secure the services of eminent members of appropriate professions in the examination of policy matters pertaining to the health of the public. The Institute acts under the responsibility given to the National Academy of Sciences by its congressional charter to be an adviser to the federal government and, upon its own initiative, to identify issues of medical care, research, and education. Dr. Kenneth I. Shine is president of the Institute of Medicine.

The National Research Council was organized by the National Academy of Sciences in 1916 to associate the broad community of science and technology with the Academy's purposes of furthering knowledge and advising the federal government. Functioning in accordance with general policies determined by the Academy, the Council has become the principal operating agency of both the National Academy of Sciences and the National Academy of Engineering in providing services to the government, the public, and the scientific and engineering communities. The Council is administered jointly by both Academies and the Institute of Medicine. Dr. Bruce M. Alberts and Dr. William A. Wulf are chairman and vice chairman, respectively, of the National Research Council.

Contents

UNCOMMON MEASURES

Equivalence and Linkage
Among Educational Tests

Public Law 105-78, enacted November 13, 1997

SEC. 306. (a) STUDY.—The National Academy of Sciences, in consultation with the National Governors' Association, the National Conference of State Legislatures, the White House, the National Assessment Governing Board, and the Congress, shall conduct a feasibility study to determine if an equivalency scale can be developed that would allow test scores from commercially available standardized tests and State assessments to be compared with each other and the National Assessment of Educational Progress.

(b) REPORT OF FINDINGS TO CONGRESS.—(1) The National Academy of Sciences shall submit a written report to the White House, the Committee on Education and the Workforce of the House of Representatives, the Committee on Labor and Human Resources of the Senate, and the Committees on Appropriations of the House of Representatives and the Senate not later than September 1, 1998.

(2) The National Academy of Sciences shall submit an interim report no later than June 15, 1998.

Executive Summary

The issues surrounding comparability and equivalency of educational assessments, although not new to the measurement and student testing literature, received broader public attention during congressional debate over the Voluntary National Tests (VNT) proposed by President Clinton in his 1997 State of the Union address. If there is any common ground shared by the advocates and opponents of national testing, it is the potential merits of bringing greater uniformity to Americans' understanding of the educational performance of their children. Advocates of the VNT argue that this is only possible through the development of a *new* test, while opponents have suggested that statistical linkages among *existing* tests might provide a basis for comparability.

To help inform this debate, Congress asked the National Research Council (NRC) to study the feasibility of developing a scale to compare, or link, scores from existing commercial and state tests to each other and to the National Assessment of Educational Progress (NAEP). This question, stated in Public Law 105-78 (November 1997), was one of three, stemming from the debate over the VNT, that the NRC was asked to study. Under the auspices of the Board on Testing and Assessment, the NRC appointed the Committee on Equivalency and Linkage of Educational Tests in January 1998.

1

KEY ISSUES

The committee faced a relatively straightforward question: Is it feasible to establish an equivalency scale that would enable commercial and state tests to be linked to one another and to the National Assessment of Educational Progress (NAEP)? The committee has reviewed research literature on the statistical and technical aspects of creating valid links between tests and on how the content, use, and purposes of educational testing in the United States influence the quality and meaning of those links. We issued an interim report in June 1998.

Testing experts have long used various statistical calculations, or linking procedures, to connect the scores from one test with those of another—in other words, to interpret a student's score on one test in terms of the scores on a test the student has not taken. A common analogy for linking tests is the formula used to convert Celsius temperatures to the Fahrenheit scale: for Americans traveling to Europe, it pays to know that 30 degrees is quite warm, not 2 degrees below freezing. Indeed, in some tightly circumscribed cases, linkage across tests is not very different. For example, equating is used to make alternate forms of the Scholastic Assessment Test (SAT) equivalent, so that college admissions officers are sure that a score of 600 means much the same thing regardless of which form of the SAT a student took (because a different form of the SAT is given at each major test administration).

But in most cases, especially those that motivate this report, linking test scores in a useful way involves more complex considerations than conversions of temperature or equating nearly identical tests across their multiple forms. For example, clusters of states are looking at possible linkages to stimulate greater comparability between scores on the state tests and between scores on the state tests and NAEP. These situations require linking tests that do not meet the strict requirements for equating and must take into account an array of complicated and complicating factors such as definition of educational goals, uses of tests, and varied emphasis on the multiplicity of skills and knowledge that comprise mastery in different subject areas.

In evaluating the feasibility of linkages, the committee focused on the linkage of various 4th-grade reading tests and the linkage of various 8th-grade mathematics tests (the topics and grades designated in the VNT proposal). We concentrated on factors that affect the validity of the inferences about student performance that users would draw from the linked test scores. We note that it is often possible to calculate arithmetic linkages that create misleading interpretations of student performance. To cite an extreme case, one could create a formula to link a reading test and a mathematics test, but the resulting scores would be ambiguous, since mathematics performance cannot be interpreted in terms of the skills used in reading. Even in less extreme situations, links between tests that differ in less dramatic ways can produce scores that are substantially misleading. Moreover, a link between two specific tests may be appropriate for one purpose, but unacceptable for others. Thus, linkage between tests involves factors that are not apparent in the analogy with linking temperature scales. These factors might be relevant whether 2 tests—or 200—are being linked. A difference between tests on any one of these factors, though not always sufficient to disqualify the proposed linkage, signals a warning about misinterpretations that may result.

ASSUMPTIONS

In approaching its charge, the committee made three key assumptions. First, the question motivating the study is predictable and sensible. It manifests a historical tension in the American educational system between a belief that curriculum, instruction, and assessment are best designed and managed at the state and local levels and a desire to bring greater uniformity to the reporting of information about student achievement in the nation's diverse educational system.

Second, though Congress was not explicit about the purposes of linkage, we recognize that the study originated in the debate over President Clinton's proposal for national tests of reading and mathematics. But the committee's charge is a narrowly defined and technical one, namely, to evaluate the feasibility of developing a scale to compare individual scores on existing tests to one another and to NAEP. Some of our findings are directly relevant to technical aspects of the VNT, for example, the requirement that it be linked to NAEP. And the committee acknowledges that a key underlying issue in the debate over the VNT is the utility of nationally comparable information on individual student achievement. However, the committee has no position on the overall merits of the VNT, and in making conclusions about the feasibility of linking existing tests we do not intend to suggest either that the nation should or should not have national tests. Neither policy decision follows inevitably from our basic conclusions about linkage and equivalency.

Third, we adopted a definition of "feasibility" that combines validity and practicality. Validity is the central criterion for evaluating any inferences based on tests and is applied in this report to inferences based on linkages among tests. By practicality we mean not only whether linkages can be calculated, in the arithmetic sense, but whether the costs of carrying out the linkages are reasonable and manageable.

CONCLUSIONS

In drawing our conclusions, the committee acknowledges that, ultimately, policy makers and educators must take responsibility for determining the degree to which they can tolerate imprecision in testing and linking. In other words: test-based decisions involve error, linkage can add to the error, and we realize that responsible people may reach different conclusions about the minimally acceptable level of precision in linkages that are intended to serve various goals. Our role is to provide science-based information on the possible sources and magnitude of the imprecision, in the hope that alerting educators and policy makers to the possibility of errors and their consequences will prove useful.

In the committee's interim report, we reached two basic conclusions:

1. Comparing the full array of currently administered commercial and state achievement tests to one another, through the development of a single equivalency or linking scale, is not feasible.

2. Reporting individual student scores from the full array of state and commercial achievement tests on the NAEP scale and transforming individual scores on these various tests and assessments into the NAEP achievement levels are not feasible.

We reached these conclusions despite our appreciation of the potential value of a technical solution to the dual challenges of maintaining diversity and innovation in testing while satisfying growing demands for nationally benchmarked data on individual student performance.

We have now considered two additional issues relevant to the committee's charge. First, we have examined whether it is feasible to link smaller subsets of tests, other than the existing "full array," and to use these linkages to make meaningful comparisons of student performance. Second, we have studied in greater depth the questions involved in reporting individual scores from any test on the NAEP scale and in terms of the NAEP achievement levels.

On these questions our level of optimism is not much higher. We find that simply reducing the number of tests under consideration does not necessarily increase the feasibility of linkage unless the tests to be linked are very similar in a number of important ways. We also find that interpreting the scores on *any* test in terms of the NAEP achievement levels poses formidable technical and interpretive challenges.

Therefore, the Committee has reached the following two additional conclusions:

3. Under limited conditions it may be possible to calculate a linkage between two tests, but multiple factors affect the validity of inferences drawn from the linked scores. These factors include the content, format, and margins of error of the tests; the intended and actual uses of the tests; and the consequences attached to the results of the tests. When tests differ on any of these factors, some limited interpretations of the linked results may be defensible while others would not.

4. Links between most existing tests and NAEP, for the purpose of reporting individual students' scores on the NAEP scale and in terms of the NAEP achievement levels, will be problematic. Unless the test to be linked to NAEP is very similar to NAEP in content, format, and uses, the resulting linkage is likely to be unstable and potentially misleading. (The committee notes that it is theoretically possible to develop an expanded version of NAEP that could be used in conducting linkage experiments, which would make it possible to establish a basis for reporting achievement test scores in terms of the NAEP achievement levels. However, the few such efforts that have been made thus far have yielded limited and mixed results.)

1

Tests and the Challenge of Linkage

Why does it matter to anyone other than testing experts whether the results of different achievement tests can be placed on a common scale? Given the vast and diverse array of educational tests used in American schools today, what purposes would be served by developing an equivalency scale to compare their results? Proponents of procedures to compare ("link") test scores argue that many Americans need more information about how individual students in the United States are performing in relation to national and international benchmarks of performance, information that is not readily available from existing tests. Moreover, they claim that parents, students, and teachers would profit from knowing how individual students' performance on key subjects compares with the performance of students in other schools, other states, and even other countries, where different tests and assessments are used. Existing tests, including the federally funded National Assessment of Educational Progress (NAEP), can now be used to compare the performance of *groups* of students, but they do not tell how *individual* students are performing relative to national and international standards. Finally, many people believe that such comparisons could spur improvements in schooling at the state and local levels (e.g., Achieve, 1998), although many other educators, testing experts, and policy makers are less enthusiastic about the utility of this type of information as a tool for genuine improvements in teaching and learning (e.g., Jones, 1997).

7

Arguments over the utility and feasibility of test score comparability, which had been limited to relatively few measurement researchers, have recently come to public attention during the debate triggered by President Clinton's proposed Voluntary National Tests (VNT). One stated goal of that initiative is to provide parents, students, and teachers with clear information about the performance of individual students as measured by national standards; one aspect of the debate centers on whether there is a need to develop a new test or an equivalency scale to link existing tests. The debate led Congress to ask the National Research Council (P.L. 105-78, November 1997), to evaluate the feasibility of developing a common scale to link scores from existing commercial and state tests to each other and to NAEP.[1]

Under the auspices of its Board on Testing and Assessment, the National Research Council established the Committee on Equivalency and Linkage of Educational Tests in January 1998. The primary focus of the committee's study is linkage among the tests currently used by states and districts to measure individual students' educational performance. We examined a substantial amount of data about selected tests that would be likely candidates for the kinds of linkage suggested in the legislation. We focused in particular on common uses of such tests, their diversity in content and format, their measurement properties, the degree to which they change over time, the extent to which state and local school policies can affect the uses and interpretations of test results, and specific properties of NAEP that enable or hinder links to other tests. We have concentrated on tests of 4th-grade reading and 8th-grade mathematics, the subjects proposed for the VNT.

BACKGROUND

Educational testing in the United States is an increasingly diverse and complex enterprise. To a large extent this situation reflects the nation's decentralized system of educational governance and the variety of choices that states and local districts have made about curriculum and assessment.

---

[1]This question is one of three stemming from the debate over the VNT, which Congress asked the National Research Council to study; for the report of the study evaluating the development of the VNT, see National Research Council (1999a); for the report of the study of appropriate test use, see National Research Council (1999c).

Over the past decade, many states and local districts have moved rapidly to revise their curriculum goals to reflect high expectations for student learning, to design customized tests aligned with those curricula, and to adopt new, test-based accountability systems aimed at bringing classroom teaching into alignment with curricular goals in order to spur improvements in teaching and learning. States are developing more content-based assessments to match curriculum goals, and those assessments differ substantially from state to state, both in content and in form. The variation occurs in part because the movement for high standards brings with it more articulation of specific content. Even within states, there is much tension over content and governance between the state and the local level. Reforms in Title I of the Improving America's Schools Act, passed in 1994, reflected and reinforced the trend toward greater state and local innovation in standard-setting, testing, and accountability. Similar patterns were articulated in the Goals 2000-Educate America Act, also passed in 1994, and the Individuals with Disabilities Education Act, passed in 1997.

At the same time, the tension of standardization versus diversity and local innovation has become manifest through the public's demand for increasingly uniform and systematic information about student performance. Educators, parents, policy makers, and others want to know more than existing tests can show about the performance of individual students. In particular, they want to know how students measure up to national and international benchmarks.

Existing tests, including NAEP, can compare the performance of *groups of students* in one state with the performance of *groups of students* in other states. International comparative assessments, such as the Third International Mathematics and Science Study (TIMSS) tell us how U.S. students *as a group* are doing compared with those in other nations. But these national programs are not designed to tell how *individual students* are performing relative to national and international standards. Despite large investments of public and private dollars in tests and testing, current tests do not readily tell us whether Leslie in Louisiana is performing as well as or better than cousin Maddie in Michigan or whether either has attained the level of mathematics skills and knowledge of Kim, who lives and attends school in Korea.

These competing trends in the testing arena—greater reliance on state and local initiatives and increased demands for national indicators of individual student performance—reflect long-standing tensions in the

American experiment with public education. The Constitution does not authorize any specific federal role in education, and the conduct of education has almost always been left to states and localities. Nonetheless, the federal government has promoted education in various ways since the founding of the republic. For example, the Northwest Ordinances of 1785 devoted public lands for the purpose of supporting education; the Morrill Act of 1862 granted land to establish "land-grant" colleges; and in 1867 Congress established a federal Office of Education to gather statistics and monitor the progress of education.

Although the concept of national education goals that are codified in law is quite recent, the federal government in the twentieth century— particularly at times of perceived international or economic crisis—has frequently turned to education as an instrument of national interests and to promote the general welfare of the nation. Often these initiatives have been controversial, causing debate over what, if any, is the proper role of the federal government in education. Today's education policy debates are in many ways a continuation of the historical experiment. Seeking ways to reconcile local variation and national standards is a manifestation of the quintessentially American ideal to build unity from respect for differences, to balance uniformity with heterogeneity—in essence, to have the best of both worlds.

Viewed through this lens of our unique experiment in pluralism and federalism, the question motivating this study is both predictable and sensible. Given the rich and increasingly diverse array of tests used by states and districts in pursuit of improved educational performance, can information be provided on a common scale? Can scores on one test be made interpretable in terms of scores on other tests? Can we have more uniform data about student performance from our healthy hodgepodge of state and local programs? Can linkage be the testing equivalent of "e pluribus unum?"

COMMITTEE'S APPROACH

In approaching our charge, the committee made a number of key assumptions. First, the question motivating this study manifests a long-standing tension in the American educational system that curriculum, instruction, and assessment are best designed and managed at the state and local levels, but that there is also a need for greater uniformity in the reporting of information about student achievement in our diverse system.

Second, though Congress was not explicit about the purposes of linkage, we recognize that the study originated in the debate over the VNT; however, we understand our charge as limited to the specific and fairly technical aspects of linkage. Though our work has some implications for possible links between the VNT and NAEP, we take no position on the overall desirability of the Voluntary National Tests. Our conclusions should not be read as either endorsing or opposing them.

Third, we adopted a definition of "feasibility" that combines validity and practicality. Validity is the central criterion for evaluating any inferences based on tests and is applied in this report to inferences based on linkages among tests. By practicality we mean not only whether linkages can be calculated, in the arithmetic sense, but whether the processes necessary to collect the data and conduct the empirical studies are reasonable and manageable.

This is the second and final report of the committee. In our interim report, published in June, we presented two important conclusions: (1) it is not feasible to develop a single scale to link the "full array" of existing tests to one another, and (2) it is not feasible to link the full array of existing tests to NAEP and report results in terms of the NAEP achievement levels. The committee reached these negative conclusions with some reluctance, given our appreciation of the potential value of a technical solution to the dual challenges of maintaining diversity and innovation in testing while satisfying growing demands for nationally benchmarked data on individual student performance.

In this final report we extend our analyses and conclusions in a number of ways. First, we consider a somewhat relaxed definition of the problem and explore issues surrounding linkages among *subsets* of existing tests. Given the apparent similarity in content, format, and purpose of at least some of the major tests used in schools today, it is reasonable to ask whether valid links among them would provide useful and accurate information to parents, students, and others. Furthermore, it is useful to consider criteria that might be applied by educators and school officials who are considering linkages across particular tests or types of tests. We also consider specific issues pertaining to NAEP, again by focusing on the validity of links between any achievement test (rather than the full array of existing tests) and the NAEP scale and achievement levels. (The NAEP achievement levels are standards that classify performance in four categories: below basic, basic, proficient, and advanced; see Chapter 3 for details.) Finally, this report provides greater detail about contextual issues that influence the feasibility of linkage, as well as elaboration of key methodological problems originally flagged in our interim report.

The rest of this chapter provides a primer on educational testing and a blueprint of the logic underlying methodological issues in test equating and linking. Chapter 2 expands the discussion of linkage by examining statistical methods, validity of links under various conditions, issues of aggregation, and criteria by which to evaluate the quality of linkages. Chapter 3 examines special issues regarding links to NAEP and the NAEP achievement levels. Chapter 4 returns to the broader policy context of this study and addresses three overlapping features of the testing "landscape" in the United States that together determine the feasibility of linkages: diversity in testing technology (test designs, formats, etc.), diversity in content emphasis across tests, and diversity in the intended and actual uses of tests in the states and districts. Chapter 5 is a synopsis of our key findings and conclusions and a brief overview of unanswered questions that may warrant further research.

DRAWING INFERENCES FROM TESTS

To evaluate the validity of inferences from scores on a given test of educational achievement—call it test A—one asks how well one can infer, from a test taker's performance on test A, the proficiencies or knowledge it is designed to measure. When scores on test A are linked to scores on a second test—call it test B—the quality of the linkage hinges on how well one can infer from performance on test B the proficiencies that test A is designed to measure. To understand what is required to create a valid linkage among tests, it is first necessary to understand the nature of tests.[2]

Tests are constructed to assess performance in a defined area of knowledge and skill, typically called a domain. In some cases, a domain may be small enough that a test can cover it exhaustively. For example, there are only a few rules governing the capitalization of nouns in English, and one could assess proficiency with them in the space of a fairly short test. Teachers frequently administer tests that cover small parts of broader

---

[2]The glossary provides definitions of terms used in this report.

domains. The achievement tests of interest to policy makers and the public, however, generally attempt to measure much larger, more diverse domains, say, 4th-grade reading or 8th-grade mathematics.

Because the time available to assess students is limited, broad domains have to be tested with small samples of those domains. Consequently, performance on the test items themselves is not as important as is the inference the scores support about mastery of the broader domains the tests are designed to measure. Missing 10 items out of 20 on a test of general vocabulary is important not because of the 10 words that were misunderstood, but because missing half of the items justifies an inference about a student's level of mastery of the thousands of words from which the test items were sampled.

Tests of the same domain can differ in important ways. In order to build a test that adequately represents its domain, a number of decisions must be made. It is helpful to think of the process as three stages leading from the domain to the final test, which can be called "framework definition," "test specification," and "item selection" (see Figure 1-1). The choices made at each stage constrain the assessment, while making it more definite.

First, the developers of an assessment must delineate, from the entire domain of the subject being assessed, such as mathematics, the scope and extent of the subdomain to be represented in the assessment. A test framework provides a detailed description of how the domain or subdomain will be represented. (As we describe in Chapter 4, differences between frameworks lead to somewhat different tests.)

Second, choices at the stage of test specification determine how a test will be built to represent the subdomain defined by the framework. Test specifications, which are sometimes called the test blueprint, specify the types and formats of the items to be used, such as the relative number of selected-response items and constructed-response items. Designers must also specify the number of tasks to be included for each part of the framework. For example, a reading test blueprint would specify the number of passages students will read. In mathematics, a blueprint would indicate that the test will include items that are best answered with the use of a numerical calculator: NAEP includes such items, but TIMSS, given in many countries, does not. The NAEP and TIMSS mathematics frameworks are very similar, yet the two assessments have different specifications about calculator use.

Third, following domain definition and test specification, test makers

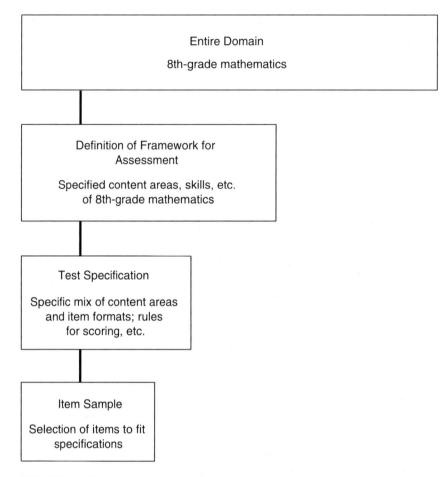

FIGURE 1-1 Decision stages in test development.

devise particular items that assess some part of the test specification. A set of items is chosen, for a given test, from a large number of prepared items, so that the selected set matches the test specification. Many testing programs have several equivalent forms of their tests in use and produce additional forms at regular intervals. For example, several forms of the Scholastic Assessment Test (SAT) are produced yearly, each of which matches the same framework and the same detailed blueprint.

DRAWING INFERENCES FROM LINKED TESTS

The choices made at each stage of test development affect the validity of a test, by which is meant the ability to use test scores to estimate proficiency in an entire domain. Linking, which in general means putting the scores from two or more tests on the same scale, magnifies the challenges to validity because different tests reflect different choices made at each stage of the test development process. Choices made during test development (as shown in Figure 1-1) lead to three basic types of linkage.

The first type of linkage adjusts scores on different forms of a test that reflect the same framework and the same test specifications. This is the case of multiple forms of the same basic test, such as the Armed Services Vocational Aptitude Battery (ASVAB), the Law School Admissions Test (LSAT), or the SAT. There is little form-to-form variation in score meaning in these circumstances. Nevertheless, the different forms contain different items, differing slightly in difficulty, so some statistical adjustment is often necessary. A linking process called "test equating" is used to make statistical adjustments of scores on each new form so that the scores on that form are comparable in meaning to scores on the previous forms.

Score distributions can sometimes be aligned by a simple linear adjustment. This method, called linear equating, is analogous to coverting temperatures between Fahrenheit and Celsius scales; see Box 1-1. Another method, equipercentile equating, adjusts for a given population the entire score distribution of one test to the entire distribution of the other. Equating permits valid inferences to be drawn from scores on any of the forms of linked tests that are built to the same specifications.

The second type of linkage is between two tests with the same framework but different test specifications. An example would be the linking of a new test, built from the NAEP frameworks but with a different mix of item types, and NAEP. The validity of inferences from such links is vulnerable to the possibility that performance of some students or groups might vary differentially across formats or other elements of the test specifications.

The committee's work has been concerned primarily with links between scores that differ in both framework and specifications. This third type of linkage is intended for tests designed to reflect different (though perhaps overlapping) perspectives of a domain.

Linking studies involving NAEP and TIMSS are examples of efforts to link assessments based on different frameworks. The potential varia-

BOX 1-1
Fahrenheit, Celsius, and Educational Tests

There is a well-known formula for linking Fahrenheit and Celsius temperatures: $F° = (9/5)C + 32°$. Thus, if one reads that Paris is suffering from a 35-degree heat wave— which may not seem very hot—one needs to multiply 35 by 9 and divide that result by 5 to get 63 and then add 32 to get a very recognizably hot 95, in degrees Fahrenheit. This formula is an example of a linking function and is analogous to what is meant by linking two test score scales. Just as one placed the Celsius value of 35 on the Fahrenheit scale and got 95 (which may be more meaningful to some people), linking can allow one to place the scores from one test on the scale of another and interpret that score or to compare it to those of test takers who took the other test. Other uses of linking assessments are to estimate how schools or districts would have performed had their students taken an assessment, such as NAEP, that they did not take.

Although the temperature measurement analogy is useful for understanding some aspects of tests, it is only a partial analogy because temperature measurement is very simple compared with the assessment of complex cognitive activities, such as reading or mathematics.

tions in assessments point to an important criterion for evaluating test-based inferences: the extent to which results are reasonably consistent across alternative measures of the same domain. For example, a given score on the NAEP grade 8 mathematics assessment is intended to measure a level of mastery of the material specified in the NAEP mathematics framework, whereas a given score on TIMSS is intended to estimate a level of mastery of the material specified by the TIMSS framework, which is overlapping, but different from the NAEP framework. Therefore, the only thing one could say with confidence is that the NAEP scores reflect mastery of the NAEP framework, and the TIMSS scores reflect mastery of the TIMSS framework. It is understandable that a student might score better on one assessment than on the other, that is, find NAEP easier than TIMSS. In practice, however, these distinctions may blur. Many users of results from a given test will interpret both scores as representing degrees of mastery of the same general domain, such as "8th-grade mathematics" and will seem perplexed at the discrepancy. It is necessary to clarify the domain to which scores should generalize in order to evaluate the quality of any linkages among tests.

Matters of test design are not the only potential factors that affect the validity of linkage-based inferences, and in some cases, they might not be the most salient. Differences in test use can also affect the interpretation of a linkage. When a test is used in a low-stakes fashion—that is, if no serious consequences are attached to scores—teachers and students may have little incentive to focus carefully on the specific sample of content reflected in the test. In contrast, when stakes are high, teachers or students have reason to care a good deal about scores, and they may focus much more on the specific sample of knowledge, skills, task types, and response expectations reflected in the specifications for that test. Thus, introduction of a new high-stakes test may lead to an increase in mastery of that part of the domain, without a corresponding improvement in mastery of other parts of the domain that the assessment is supposed to represent but does not. This narrowed instructional focus may produce inflated scores on that high-stakes test. Whatever this focus might imply for the validity of the measured gains, however, it is likely to throw into question the stability over time of any linkage between the high-stakes test and any low-stakes test of the same domain.

Since all tests are small samples from broad and complex domains, a possible lack of consistency across measures is an omnipresent threat to linkage that warrants careful, case-by-case evaluation; see Box 1-2 for a discussion of linking methods.

BOX 1-2
Linking Methods

Equating. The strongest kind of linking, and the one with the most technical support, is equating. Equating is most frequently used when comparing the results of different forms of a single test that have been designed to be parallel. The College Board equates different forms of the Scholastic Assessment Test (SAT) and treats the results as interchangeable. Equating is possible if test content, format, purpose, administration, item difficulty, and populations are equivalent.

In linear equating, the mean and standard deviation of one test is adjusted so that it is the same as the mean and standard deviation of another. Equipercentile equating adjusts the entire score distribution of one test to the entire score distribution of the other for a given population. In this case, scores at the same percentile on two different test forms are equivalent. Thus, if a score of 122 on one test, A, is at the 75th percentile and a score of 257 on another test, B, is also at the 75th percentile for the same population of test takers, then 122 and 257 are linked by the equipercentile method. This means that 75 percent of the test takers in this population would score 122 or less on test A or would score 257 or less on test B. The linked scores, 122 and 257, have the same meaning in this very specific and widely used sense, and we would place the A score of 122 onto the scale of test B by using the value of 257 for it. By following this procedure for each percentile value from 1 to 99, tests A and B are linked.

Two tests can also be equated using a third test as an anchor. This anchor test should have similar content to the original tests, although it is typically shorter than the two original tests. Often the anchor test is a separately timed section of the original tests. Sometimes, however, the items on the anchor test are interspersed with the items on the main tests. A separate score is computed for the responses to those items as if they were a separate test. An assumption of the equipercentile equating methodology is that the linking function found in this manner is consistent across the various populations that could be chosen for the equating. For example, the same linking function should be obtained if the population is restricted only to boys or only to girls. However, the research literature shows that this consistency is to be expected only when the tests being linked are very similar in a variety of ways that are discussed in the rest of this report.

Calibration. Tests or assessments that are constructed for different purposes, using different content frameworks or test specifications, will almost always violate the conditions required for equating. When scores from two different tests are put on the same scale, the results are said to be comparable, or calibrated. Most of the statistical methods used in equating can be used in calibration, but it is not expected that the results will be consistent across different populations.

Two types of empirical data support equating and calibration of scores between two tests. In one type, the two tests are given to a single group of test takers. When the same group takes both tests, the intercorrelation of the tests provides some empirical evidence of equivalent content. In a second design, two tests are given to equivalent groups of test takers. Equivalent groups are often formed by giving both tests at the same time to a large group, with some of the examinees taking one test and some the other. When the tests are given at different times to different groups of test takers, equivalence is harder to assert.

Two tests can be equated or calibrated using a third test as an anchor. This method requires that one group of students takes tests A and C, while another group takes tests B and C. Tests A and B are then calibrated through the anchor test, C. For this method to be valid, the anchor test should have the same content as the original tests, although it is typically shorter than the other tests.

One relatively new equating procedure, used extensively in NAEP and many other large testing programs, depends on the ability to calibrate the individual items that make up a test, rather than the test itself. Each of a large number of items about a given subject is related or calibrated to a scale measuring that subject, using a statistical theory called item response theory (IRT). The method works only when the items are all assessing the same material and requires that a large number of items be administered to a large representative set of test takers. Once all items are calibrated, a test can be formed from a subset of the items with the assurance that it can be automatically equated to another test formed from a selection of different items.

Projection. A special unidirectional form of linking can be used to predict or "project" scores on one test from scores on another test without any expectation that exactly the same things are being measured. Usually, both tests are given to a sample of students and then statistical regression methods are applied. It is important to note that projecting test A onto test B gives different results from projecting test B onto test A.

Moderation. Moderation is the weakest form of linking. It is used when the tests have different blueprints and are given to different, nonequivalent groups of examinees. Procedures that match distributions using scores are called statistical moderation links, while others that match distributions using judgments are called social moderation links. In either case, the resulting links are only valid for making some very general comparisons (Mislevy, 1992; Linn, 1993).

2

Technical Aspects of Links

Throughout this report we use the term "linkage" to mean various well-established statistical methods (see, e.g., Mislevy, 1992; Linn, 1993) for connecting scores on different tests and assessments with each other and for reporting them on a common scale. In this chapter we explain how linkage works.

Because the technical aspects of testing are unfamiliar to many readers of this report, analogies with measuring temperature may be useful. For one thing, like test results, temperatures are reported on scales that are somewhat arbitrary, such as the 32-212 degrees of the Fahrenheit scale and the 0-500 scale for the National Assessment of Educational Progress (NAEP). Points on each scale represent a quality of what is being measured: 95 degrees Fahrenheit is hot; a 350 NAEP score is high performance. Different temperature scales, say, Fahrenheit and Celsius, can be linked by using a simple formula. In that way, one would know that 30 degrees Celsius is hot, not 2 degrees colder than freezing.

Whether one is discussing links of temperature or scores from different tests, a linkage provides a method for adjusting the results from one instrument to be comparable with another instrument. In some cases, a student's score on one test can be adjusted and then substituted for a score from a test not taken by the student. In other cases, only aggregate or group-level results can be linked and compared; for example, the average reading proficiency of 4th-grade students in Maine compared with those in Vermont, derived from different tests.

In the case of the Fahrenheit and Celsius scales, the linkage or formula for converting a temperature value from one scale to the other is exact; for example, 35 degrees Celsius is always equivalent to 95 degrees Fahrenheit. In contrast, linking different educational assessments is not exact. As noted in Chapter 1, different testing instruments may purport to assess similar general domains but may place differing emphases on specific aspects of these domains. Even when the content and format of tests are perfectly aligned, any linkage between them can only be estimated and, therefore, will always contain at least some estimation error. The rest of this chapter discusses approaches that have been used to link educational assessments and the problems one might encounter, or the potential problems one should try to uncover, in such linking.

CONSTRUCTING LINKS

Statistical Methods for Linking

Most linking methods are based on statistical analyses of the score distributions on the tests or test forms being linked. Various study designs can be used to collect the data needed for linking. A common method is the single-group design, in which a single group of people takes both tests or test forms. In this design, the intercorrelation of the tests provides some empirical evidence of the extent to which the two tests have equivalent content. However, the single-group design has the disadvantage that each student must take two tests: fatigue may affect the scores on the second test, some part of the first test may suggest how to answer an item on the second test, or there may be a large time lag between the two test administrations.

A second method for collecting data for linking is an equivalent-group design. In the equivalent-group design, two tests are given to equivalent groups of test takers. Equivalent groups are often formed by giving both tests at the same time to a large group, with one randomly selected half of the examinees taking one test and the remaining half taking the other. When the tests are given at different times to different groups of test takers, the equivalence of the two groups is harder to guarantee.

A third method for collecting data for linking involves an anchor test.

Two tests can be equated or calibrated using a third test as an anchor. This method requires that one group of students takes tests A and C, while another group takes tests B and C. Tests A and B can then be linked through various statistical computations involving the anchor test, C. For this method to be valid, the anchor test has to have the same content as the original tests, although it is typically shorter, and therefore less reliable than the other tests.

Forms of Linking

Despite efforts by Mislevy (1992) and Linn (1993) to bring coherence to the definitions of linking, the literature is not completely consistent in the use of the terminology. The term equating is often used generally; in this report we use the term linking as the general term. Many of the statistical methods are applicable to all forms of linking, but some are applicable only for some types of linking. This section defines and discusses equating, calibration, projection, and moderation as used in this report.

Equating   The term equating is reserved for situations in which two or more different forms of a single test have been constructed according to the same blueprint—that is, the forms adhere to the same test specifications, are of about the same difficulty and reliability, are given under the same standardized conditions, and are to be used for the same purposes (see e.g., Holland and Rubin, 1982; Kolen and Brennan, 1995). In linear equating, the scores on one test are adjusted so that the mean and standard deviation of the scores are the same as the mean and standard deviation of the other test. Equipercentile equating adjusts the entire score distribution of one test to the entire score distribution of the other, so that scores at the same percentile on two different test forms are equivalent.

Calibration   If two assessments have the same framework but have different test specifications (including differing lengths) and different statistical characteristics, then linking the scores for comparability is called calibration. Sometimes a short form of a test is used for screening purposes: its scores are calibrated with the scores from the long form. Sometimes tests designed for different grade levels are calibrated to a common scale; this process is also called vertical equating.

A common calibration approach is to apply item response theory (IRT) methods to obtain individual proficiency values for the common domain being measured. The IRT procedure, used extensively in NAEP and many other large testing programs, depends on the ability to calibrate the individual items that make up a test, rather than the test itself. Each of a large number of items in a given domain is related or calibrated to a scale measuring that subject, using IRT methods. This method is applicable only when the items are all assessing the same material, and it requires that a large number of items be administered to a large and representative group of test takers, generally using some variant of the anchor test data collection design. After all the items are calibrated, a test can be formed from a subset of the items, and it will then equate automatically to another test formed from a selection of different items.

Projection A special unidirectional form of linking can be used to predict or project scores on one test from scores on another test, without any expectation that the same things are being measured. The single-group data collection design is required, and statistical regression methods are used. It is important to note that projecting test A onto test B gives different results from projecting test B onto test A. Also, the distribution of scores projected from test A onto test B will have a smaller standard deviation than the actual scores on test B. For these reasons, projection is not used in the strict equating of test forms.

Moderation Moderation is the weakest form of linking, used for tests with different specifications that are given to different, nonequivalent groups of examinees. Procedures that match distributions using scores are called statistical moderation links; procedures that match distributions using judgments are called social moderation links. Social moderation generally relies on information external to the testing situation. In either case, the resulting links are only valid for making some very general comparisons (Mislevy, 1992; Linn, 1993).

Examples

Major tests, such as the Armed Services Vocational Aptitude Battery (ASVAB), the Scholastic Assessment Test (SAT) , the American College Test (ACT), the Law School Admissions Test (LSAT), use the same blueprint for all forms of their tests. New forms are regularly equated with past forms, so that the scores on any form mean the same as the scores on any other form in the series. Many statistical methods can be used for equating. Because of the routine nature of equating and its unambiguous meaning in the appropriate circumstances, this type of linking is not discussed further in this report.

There are several situations in which it is fairly routine for two tests to be linked and the results of the linkage to be used for well-defined purposes. For example, when a new edition of a test is introduced into a product line, a test publisher will establish links between the new edition and the old one so that results obtained from the two tests can be compared. For example, CTB/McGraw Hill linked the California Test of Basic Skills with its newer TerraNova test; Harcourt Brace Educational Measurement linked the Stanford Achievement Test 8th Edition with the Stanford Achievement Test 9th Edition; Riverside Publishing linked the Iowa Tests of Basic Skills M with earlier editions of the test. Sometimes the test specifications may have changed in response to shifts in educational emphases, and the old and new editions will not be as similar as two different forms of a test made to the same specifications; however, old and new editions generally can be calibrated successfully and put on the same scale.

Another routine use of linking occurs when states or schools change from one publisher's testing program to another. In these cases it is not uncommon for the publisher of the new test to conduct a study to link the two testing programs (Wendy Yen, personal communication). For example, in 1997 the state of Virginia switched from one commercial test, the ITBS, to another, the Stanford 9. To effect the switch smoothly, the scores on the two achievement tests were linked, using a same-group linking design. The tests in some subjects were judged to have such different content that a link would not be meaningful, but in mathematics, reading, and language, the content was sufficiently similar that a link would be useful. For example, a correlation of .81 was found between the two tests of 8th-grade mathematics for a representative sample of 596 students. This correlation is high, but it still indicates some substantive differences between the two tests. The results of the linking were checked by comparing the observed performance on the 1996-1997 administration of the Stanford 9 with the performance that was predicted on the basis of scores from the 1995-1996 administration of the ITBS (Virginia Department of Education, 1997). The correspondence at the state level was high in spite of substantial variation at the district level.

In 1972 and 1973, at the request of Congress, the Anchor Test Study (Loret et al., 1972, 1973; Bianchini et al., 1974, 1975) was undertaken to link eight major commercial achievement tests. The purpose of the study was to measure student achievement gains regardless of the test that they took, in order to evaluate the impact of Title I of the Elementary and Secondary Education Act. Reading was chosen because of its centrality in Title I and because it was expected to permit linkages more easily than other subjects. The study provided nationally representative norms on these tests and also developed equivalence tables so that a student's standardized reading score on any one of the tests could be put on a single scale. Technically, all tests in the study were calibrated to the scale of the Metropolitan Achievement Test (MAT), using linear or equipercentile procedures. The results indicated that the tests could be linked sufficiently closely that they produced comparable scores on vocabulary and reading comprehension. Although the anchor test study was obsolete by the time it was released, primarily because of changes in the tests, it remains a model of linkage development.

A proposal for a similar study was recently made for use in the assessment of California schools. The proposed study would have enabled a local school district to assess student achievement with any of a list of acceptable commercial tests; the tests would be linked to each other as were the tests in the Anchor Test Study. Results on the achievement tests, aggregated for the students in a school, would be used to rate the performance of each school. However, many experts said that satisfactory links could not be developed among the available commercial tests (Haertel, 1996; Yen, 1996), partly because today's achievement tests differ more in content and format than did the reading tests in the 1970s (see also Chapter 4). Many feared that because schools could earn financial rewards for high scores, districts could manipulate the system by selecting the test that most closely conformed to their curriculum. Ultimately, the plan was scrapped; instead, a single commercial test was chosen for use in the entire state.

Another study linked the MAT to the Connecticut Mastery Test in mathematics (Behuniak and Tucker, 1992). The MAT, which offers separate versions for grades 4, 6, and 8, was chosen as the commercial achievement test series that most closely matched Connecticut's curriculum objectives. In each grade, a sample of students took both the appropriate MAT and the Connecticut tests. The link was apparently determined by statistical moderation and was evaluated by using an index based on the correlation of the two tests, as proposed by Gulliksen (1950). The study reported that the two tests were as highly correlated as possible, given their respective reliabilities. This study is similar in many respects to the Anchor Test Study. Unfortunately, the authors did not report detailed analyses of the scores, such as subgroup analyses or other evaluations. Table 2-1 presents summaries of prior linkage studies.

COMMON PROBLEMS IN LINKS

If two tests (A and B) measure different aspects of the performance of the examinees, either because they measure different domains or because they measure the same domain differently, then the examinees are likely to exhibit different patterns of proficiency on the tests. Thus, the scores on test A will not provide accurate and unbiased estimates of scores on test B. As noted in Chapter 1, the domains of reading and mathematics are large: two tests of 4th-grade reading may measure different arrays of skills and knowledge, and an individual student may perform very differently on them. Linking the scores between the tests would have little utility.

A difference in overall reliability is also troublesome in linking tests. It is desirable that tests being linked have errors of measurement of similar magnitude at equivalent score points. If two tests differ in reliability, then their scores should not be used interchangeably. Calibration or projection can be used to link unequally reliable tests for some purposes, but the linked scores must be interpreted with great care. Scores from the less reliable test will still have a large margin of error, even if reported on the scale of the more reliable test. Some test users may ignore the larger margin of error and misinterpret the scores.

When linking forms of a single test, forms with different reliability cannot be equated. Strict equating requires that it should be a matter of indifference to a test taker which of two equated test forms is used. The lore of equating holds that test takers who have a choice of two forms and who expect to do poorly should, if they are willing to take a chance, choose the less reliable form, for there is a greater chance of getting an unrealistically high score by chance on that form, because of its larger margin of error. Of course there is also a greater chance of getting an unrealistically low score on the same form, but some may be willing to take that chance. No such gamesmanship is possible with equally reliable test forms. This colorful description of the dilemma is widely quoted (see, e.g., Lord and Novick, 1968; Peterson et al., 1993) and is intended to force consideration of the more likely situation in which test takers have no choice and may have to take the less reliable test form.

Differences in item and response formats or in administration can also affect the validity of a linkage. In some cases, seemingly small changes in conditions can have large effects. For example, in 1984, several changes were made in NAEP's method of measuring reading, with important effects on the results: the 1986 results showed large losses in performance among 9- and 17-year-olds. A series of studies of the "NAEP reading anomaly" found a number of very small effects, none of which, by itself, could have caused the problem, but which together made a substantial change (Beaton and Zwick, 1990).

Context effects may also arise in which the difficulty or reliability of a test or block of items is affected by preceding tests or blocks of items (see, e.g., Williams et al., 1995). Some format changes, such as those between paper-and-pencil and computer-based testing, have so far shown little effect on what tests measure or the ways they can be linked (Mead and Dragow, 1993). Other format changes, such as those between hands-on and computer-simulated performance tasks, show large differences (Shavelson et al., 1992). Since linkage problems may or may not arise when tests to be linked have different formats, prudence suggests that attention be given to format issues in linkage.

Differences in the context of test administration, which include the consequences associated with test outcomes (the stakes), are widely believed to affect the stability of test linkages over time. For example, in both Kentucky and North Carolina, where the relationship between the state assessment and NAEP has been examined, there is evidence that scores have improved somewhat more on the state assessments than on NAEP. This effect suggests that as the activities in the classroom become more in line, over time, with the state's intended curriculum, and more aligned with the constructs measured by a state's assessment, the state assessment will become, in effect, easier for each successive cohort of students. However, for NAEP there is no corresponding change in curriculum or instruction in the classroom (because it is a low-stakes test), and its difficulty remains essentially the same over time. The result is that a linkage between state assessment and NAEP that is established at or near the introduction of sanctions or rewards associated with the state assessment, will become out of date and inaccurately reflect equivalent performance on the state assessment and NAEP over time. This effect

TABLE 2-1 Abridged Summaries of Prior Linkage Research

Study	Purpose
The Anchor Test Study (Loret et al., 1972, 1973)	To develop an equivalency scale to compare reading test results for Title I program evaluation. The study was sponsored by a $1,000,000 contract with the U.S. Office of Education.
Projecting to the NAEP Scale: Results from the North Carolina End-of-Grade Testing Program (Williams et al., 1995)	To link a comprehensive state achievement test to the NAEP scale for mathematics so that the more frequently administered state tests could be used for purposes of monitoring progress of North Carolina students with respect to national achievement standards.

Methodology	Key Findings
Number of participants: 200,000 students for norming phase; 21 sample groups of approximately 5,000 students each for the equating phase.	Tests with similar content can be linked together with reasonable accuracy.
Eight tests, representing almost 90 percent of reading tests being administered in the states at that time, were selected for the study.	Relationships between tests were determined to be reasonably similar for male and female students but not for racial groups.
Participants took two tests.	The equivalency scale was accurate for individuals but aggregated results,
Created new national norms for one test and, through equating, all eight tests.	e.g., school or district, would have increased error stemming from combining results.
Administered different combinations of standardized reading tests to different subjects taking into account the need to balance demographic factors and instructional differences.	Every time a new test is introduced the procedure has to be replicated for that test.
	The stability of the linkage has to be reestablished regularly because instruction on one test but not on others can invalidate the linkage.
A total of 2,824 students from 99 schools were tested using 78 items from a short form of the North Carolina End-of-Grade Test and two blocks of released 1992 NAEP items that were embedded in the test.	A satisfactory linkage was obtained for statewide statistics as a whole that were accurate enough to predict NAEP means or quartile distributions with only modest error.
Test booklets were spiraled so that some students took NAEP items first, others took North Carolina End-of-Grade Test items first.	The linkages had to be adjusted separately by from 0.1 to 0.2 standard deviations for different ethnic groups, demonstrating that the linking was inappropriate for predicting individual scores from the North Carolina Test to the NAEP scale.
The final linkage to the NAEP scale used projection. Scores from the NAEP blocks were determined from student responses using NAEP parameters but not the conditioning analysis used by NAEP. Regular scores from the North Carolina test were used.	The following were considered important factors in establishing a strong link: content on the North Carolina Test was closely aligned with state curriculum and NAEP's was not; student performance was affected by the order of the items in their test booklets; motivation or fatigue affected performance for some students.

TABLE 2-1   (*Continued*)

Study	Purpose
Linking Statewide Tests to NAEP (Ercikan, 1997)	To examine the accuracy of linking statewide test results to NAEP by comparing the results of four states' assessment programs with the NAEP results for those states.
Toward World-Class Standards: A Research Study Linking International and National Assessments (Pashley and Phillips, 1993)	To pilot test a method for obtaining accurate links between the International Assessment of Educational Progress (IAEP) and NAEP so that other countries can be compared with the United States, bothnationally and at the state level, in terms of NAEP performance standards.

Methodology	Key Findings
Compared each state's assessment data to their NAEP data using equipercentile comparisons of score distributions. Since none of the four states used exactly the same form of the California Achievement Test for their state testing program, state results had to be converted to a common scale. This scale was developed by the publisher of the California Achievement Test series.	The link from separate tests to NAEP varies from one state to the next with effect sizes ranging from 0.18 to 0.6 standard deviation. It was not possible to determine whether the state-to-state differences were due to the different test(s), the moderate content alignment, the motivation of the students, or the nature of the student population. Linking state tests to NAEP (by matching distributions) is so imprecise that results should not be used for high-stakes purposes.
A sample of 1,609 U.S. 8th-grade students were assessed with both IAEP and NAEP instruments in 1992 to establish a link between these assessments. Based on test results from the sample testing, the relationships between IAEP and NAEP proficiency estimates were investigated. Projection methodology was used to estimate the percentages of students from the 20 countries, assessed with the IAEP, who could perform at or above the three performance levels established for NAEP. Various sources of statistical error were assessed.	Differences of proportions of students basic or above, proficient or above, and advanced ranged from 0.01 to 0.03, corresponding to differences of 0.1 to 0.10 standard deviation on the NAEP scale. The methods researchers use to establish links between tests (at least partially) determine how valid the link is for drawing particular inferences about performance. Establishing this link required a sample of students who took both assessments. It is possible to establish an accurate statistical link between the IAEP and NAEP, but policy makers, among others, should proceed with caution when interpreting results from such a link. IAEP and NAEP were fairly similar in construction and scoring, which made linking easier. The effects of unexplored sources of nonstatistical error, such as motivation levels, were not determined.

TABLE 2-1   (Continued)

Study	Purpose
Comparing the NAEP Trial State Assessment Results with the IAEP International Results (Beaton and Gonzalez, 1993)	To determine how American students compare to foreign students in mathematics, and how well foreign students meet the mathematics standards of the National Assessment Governing Board (NAGB).
Linking to a Large-Scale Assessment: An Empirical Evaluation (Bloxom et al., 1995)	To compare the mathematics achievement of new military recruits with the general U.S. student population, using a link between the Armed Services Vocational Aptitude Battery (ASVAB) and NAEP. The emphasis of the study was to provide and illustrate an approach for empirically evaluating the statistical accuracy of such a linkage.

Methodology	Key Findings
At that time data were not available for examinees that took both assessments; therefore they relied on a simple distribution-matching procedure.	Moderation procedures are sensitive to age/grade differences.
Rescaled scores to produce a common mean and standard deviation on the two tests.	IAEP and NAEP have many similarities but are not identical and differ in some significant ways.
Translated IAEP scores into NAEP scores by aligning the means and standard deviations for the two tests.	Results of the linking were different for countries with high average IAEP scores.
Transformed the IAEP scores for students in the IAEP samples in each participating country into equivalent NAEP scores.	Different methods of linking IAEP and NAEP can produce different results, and further study is necessary to determine which method is best.
A sample of 8,239 applicants for military service were administered an operational ASVAB and a NAEP survey in 1992. These applicants were told that there were no stakes attached to the NAEP survey.	Statistically, an accurate distribution of recruit achievement can be found by projecting onto the NAEP scale.
ASVAB scores were projected on the NAEP scale in mathematics to allow for comparison between the achievement of military applicants with the general U.S. population of 12th grade students.	A comparison of the link from ASVAB to NAEP showed differences on the order of .02 standard deviation.
Statistical checks were made by constructing the link separately for low-scoring candidates and for high-scoring candidates.	Doubt was cast on the validity of the link because factors related to motivation may have underestimated the assessment-based proficiency distribution of recruits in this study, meaning that in spite of the statistical precision of the linkage, the resulting estimates may not be valid for practical purposes.

TABLE 2-1   (Continued)

Study	Purpose
The Potential of Criterion-Referenced Tests with Projected Norms (Behuniak and Tucker, 1992)	To determine if norm-referenced scores could be provided, for the purpose of Chapter 1 program evaluation, by linking the Connecticut Mastery Test, a criterion-referenced test closely aligned with state curriculum, and a national "off-the-shelf" norm-referenced achievement test. The purpose of the linking was to meet federal guidelines for Chapter 1 reporting without requiring students to take two tests.

Methodology	Key Findings
Compared two tests, the Metropolitan Achievement Test 6 (MAT 6) and the Stanford Achievement Test 7 (SAT 7) to determine which was more closely aligned with state content standards. Selected the MAT 6 for the study. For a relevant population, calibrated the items from the two instruments in a given subject as a single IRT calibration then used the results to calibrate the tests. Linked results using equipercentile equating. Examined changes over two years to check the stability of the link.	There were enough content differences between the two norm-referenced tests and the Connecticut Mastery Test to decide which test would make a better, if not perfect, candidate for linking to the state test than the other. It was possible to develop a link between the MAT 6 and the Connecticut Mastery Test that accurately predicted Normal Curve Equivalent scores for the MAT 6 from the Connecticut Mastery Test, but no good validity checks were used. The linking function changed somewhat over time and the authors believed that this divergence would continue because teachers were gearing instruction to state standards which were more closely aligned with the Connecticut Mastery Test than the MAT 6. Thus, the linking would have to be reestablished regularly to remain valid for the purposes that it was intended to serve.

TABLE 2-1   (Continued)

Study	Purpose
Linking Statewide Tests to the National Assessment of Educational Progress: Stability of Results (Linn and Kiplinger, 1995)	To investigate the adequacy of linking statewide standardized test results to the National Assessment of Educational Progress (NAEP) to allow for accurate comparisons between state academic performance and the national performance levels measured by NAEP.

Methodology	Key Findings
Obtained two years (1990 and 1992) results from four states' testing programs and corresponding results from the NAEP Trial State Assessment for the same 2 years. (Standardized tests used in the four states were different.) Used equipercentile equating procedures to compare data from state tests and NAEP. The standardized test results were converted to the NAEP scale using the 1990 data and resulting conversion tables were then applied to the 1992 data. Examined content match between standardized tests and NAEP and reanalyzed data using subsections of the standardized tests and NAEP.	The link could estimate average state performance on NAEP but was not accurate for scores at the top or bottom of the scale. At the lower range of the scale the difference was about 10 points on the NAEP scale, or about 0.3 standard deviation. The equating function diverged for males and females, meaning that NAEP scores for a state would have been over-predicted if the equating function for males was used rather than the equating function for females. The consistency of the linkage was examined over 2 years. They found differences of from 0.0 to 0.15 standard deviation from 1990 to 1992. Linking standardized tests to NAEP using equipercentile equating procedures is not sufficiently trustworthy to use for other than rough approximations. Designing tests in accordance with a common framework might make linking more feasible.

TABLE 2-1   (*Continued*)

Study	Purpose
Using Performance Standards to Link Statewide Achievement Results to NAEP (Waltman, 1997)	To investigate the comparability of performance standards obtained by using both statistical and social moderation to link NAEP standards to the Iowa Tests of Basic Skills (ITBS).

Methodology	Key Findings
Compared 1992 NAEP Trial State Assessment with ITBS for Iowa 4th-grade public school students. Used two different types of linking for separate facets of the study. A socially moderated linkage was obtained by setting standards independently on the ITBS using the same achievement-level descriptions used to set the NAEP achievement levels. An equipercentile procedure was used to establish a statistically moderated link.	For students who took both assessments, the corresponding achievement regions on the NAEP and ITBS scales produced low to moderate percents of agreement in student classification. Agreement was particularly low for students at the advanced level; two-thirds or more were classified differently. Cut-scores on the ITBS scale, established by moderation, were lower than those used by NAEP resulting in more students being classified as basic, proficient, or advanced on the ITBS than estimated by NAEP, possibly due to content and skills-standards mismatch between the ITBS and NAEP. The equipercentile linkage was reasonably invariant across types of communities, in terms of percentages of students classified at each level. Regardless of the method used to establish the ITBS cut-scores or the criteria used to classify students, the inconsistency of student-level match limits even many inferences about group performance.

TABLE 2-1   (*Continued*)

Study	Purpose
Study of the Linkages of 1996 NAEP and State Mathematics Assessments in Four States (McLaughlin, 1998)	To address the need for clear, rigorous standards for linkage; to provide the foundation for developing practical guidelines for states to use in linking state assessments to NAEP; and to demonstrate that it is important for educational policy makers to be aware that linkages that support one use may not be valid for another.
The Maryland School Performance Assessment Program: Performance Assessment with Psychometric Quality Suitable for High Stakes Usage (Yen and Ferrara, 1997)	To compare the Maryland State Performance Assessment Program (MSPAP) with the Comprehensive Test of Basic Skills (CTBS) in order to establish the validity of the state test in reference to national norms.

Methodology	Key Findings
A sample of four states that had participated in the 1996 state NAEP mathematics assessment and whose state assessment mathematics tests could potentially be linked to NAEP at the individual student level participated in this study. Participating states used different assessments in their state testing programs. There were eight linkage samples, ranging in size from 1,852 to 2,444 students. Study matched students who participated in the NAEP assessment in their states with their scores on the state assessment instrument, using projection with multilevel regression.	Linked scores had a 95 percent confidence interval of almost 2.0 standard deviations, which were not sufficiently accurate to permit reporting individual student proficiency on NAEP based on the state assessment score. Links differed noticeably by minority status and school district, in all four states. Students with the same state assessment score would be projected to have different standings on the NAEP proficiency scale, depending on their minority status and school district.
Compared results from a group of 5th-grade students who took both MSPAP and CTBS— correlations were obtained. The intent was to establish the validity of MSPAP so a link was not obtained.	Intercorrelations of the two tests indicated that the two measures were assessing somewhat different aspects of achievement.

TABLE 2-1   (Continued)

Study	Purpose
Linking the National Assessment of Educational Progress and the Third International Mathematics and Science Study: Eighth Grade Results (National Center for Education Statistics, 1998)	To provide useful information about the performance of states relative to other countries. The study broadly compares state 8th-grade mathematics and science performance for each of 44 states and jurisdictions participating in NAEP with the 41 nations that participated in the Third International Mathematics and Science Study (TIMSS).

will result in inaccurate predictions of what NAEP performance would be based on the results of the later state assessments.

EVALUATING LINKS

How can one evaluate the quality of a link? How small can the effects of any particular problem be that will invalidate the linkage? How large can the effects be and still permit a useful linkage? The answers to these questions depend on how the linked scores will be used and what inferences will be drawn. The basic question is: If one administers test A and uses the results to infer what the results on test B would have been, will those inferred results produce the same interpretations as would have resulted if test B had been administered?

Methodology	Key Findings
The study provides predicted TIMSS results for 44 states and jurisdictions, based on their actual NAEP results.	For one state (Minnesota), an excellent link was obtained for 8th-grade mathematics and science. Percentages of students actually scoring in the top 10 percent and in the top 50 percent internationally were within 2 to 5 percent of results predicted by the NAEP-TIMSS link. The 4th-grade results and results in other states have yet to be released, so the evaluation of the NAEP-TIMSS link must be considered incomplete.
A statistically moderated link was used to establish the link between NAEP and TIMSS based on applying formal linear equating procedures.	
The link was established using reported results from the 1995 administration of TIMSS in the United States and the 1996 NAEP and matching characteristics of the score distributions for the two assessments.	
Validated the linking functions using data provided by states that participated in both state-level NAEP and state-level TIMSS but were not included in the development of the original linking function.	

This section considers general empirical approaches to the evaluation of linkages. Specific evaluations should also examine the match in the contexts of the tests, and content experts should assess the degree to which tests measure the same domain.

General Considerations

To evaluate a link, one should first clearly define the objectives and purposes that the link will serve. Will the link compare individual student performance or group performance or both? How long will the link be in effect? Will subgroup differences be considered? These objectives and purposes, or stated uses, should guide the evaluation of the quality of the link, including estimating the size of possible statistical errors and assessing the link's robustness to changes over time.

How Accurate Must the Linkage Be?　Developers of a linkage should set targets for the level of accuracy that will be required to support its stated uses. An example might be: "We want to compare mean student performance in two districts using different assessments. We would like the standard error of the district B mean projected onto the scale used by district A to be less than .05 standard deviations." Another example might be: "We want to know whether an individual student taking assessment B is achieving at or above the proficient level on NAEP, and we want this classification to be correct for at least 95 percent of the students who take assessment B."

Over What Subgroups Must the Linkage Be Stable?　In specifying intended uses, linkage developers should describe the different units (states, districts, schools, and individual students) that will be compared with each other or with fixed standards. It is important to understand the ways in which these units might differ and how that could affect the linkage between the two tests. For example, states might use different curricula, which could affect the linkage. If the students in one state are exposed to a curriculum that is more aligned with test A than test B, they will probably score relatively better on test A than will students from another state, where the curriculum does not favor test A. If the linkage from test A to test B is developed on students from the first state and then applied to students in the second state, there will be a constant bias, underestimating the test B performance of students from the second state on the basis of their test A performance. Such a bias could lead to significant error, even in estimating aggregate means. Since the bias is present for all students, the size of the error will not decrease as the sample size increases.

When a linkage is to be used with scores for individual students, it is particularly difficult to identify the relative dimensions over which the linkage must be stable. Students differ in many ways (e.g., preparation, motivation, curricular exposure, and other background characteristics) that can differentially affect scores on the two tests being linked. The linkage must be stable across all of these characteristics for the linked individual results to be valid.

What Data Are Needed?　To assess the accuracy and stability of a linkage and thus determine, empirically, whether a given linkage is adequate to support its intended uses, the first step is to gather evidence of the relationship of the scores from the two tests. Such evidence provides an indication of the degree to which the two tests measure the same domain (or the correlation of the different domains measured by the two tests). The evidence will also provide an indication of the relative accuracy (reliability and measurement error) with which each test measures its underlying domain.

In all cases, empirical data are required to establish a linkage, and the same data can provide much useful information on the accuracy and stability of the linkage. In most cases, additional data are required to determine stability over time or over variation in other factors on which the two tests differ (e.g., administration conditions; use; subgroup membership; and examinee motivation, differential preparation, or exposure to curriculum).

Sample Designs

Two Tests

As noted above, the most direct method for establishing and evaluating a linkage is the single-group design, in which two tests are administered to a common set of examinees. In designing a single-group data collection, the following design issues should be addressed:

• The same conditions of administration should be followed for each test insofar as possible. These include time of year, factors (such as use) that affect student motivation, test length, and breaks.
• The two samples should include sufficient numbers of examinees from the different groups across which the linkage is to apply.
• Adequate sample size should be obtained both overall and for each examinee group to be analyzed separately. Sample size requirements will depend on the accuracy targets of the linkage. The power to detect key differences and the standard error of relevant estimates should be determined in advance.

Once a linkage study has been designed and the data have been collected, several analyses should be performed:

• Examine the data for outliers that could distort results using scatterplots or other means. Eliminate discrepant cases if necessary.

- Estimate score reliability for each test.
- Determine the correlation between the observed (estimated) scores for the two tests. Also examine the "disattenuated" correlation—that is, an estimation of the underlying true scores, adjusting for the fact that the observed score correlation is attenuated due to lack of perfect reliability of either of the two measures.
- Examine the linearity of the relationship of the two tests through examination of scatterplots or by fitting regression equations with nonlinear terms and examining the significance of the coefficients for the nonlinear terms.
- Establish the overall linkage. If the relationship is linear and the score distributions have approximately the same shape, linear linking can be used; otherwise, equiperentile linking is preferred. If the projection method is chosen, ordinary regression methods can be used.
- Estimate linkage error. Various estimation errors in statistical linking have been identified in previous linking studies. For example, Pashley and Phillips (1993) and Johnson and Siegendorf (National Center for Education Statistics, 1998) attempted to determine the size of potential statistical errors due to regression estimation, sample-to-population estimation, design effects, and measurement error. The types and sizes of linkage errors will depend on the design of the linking study.
- Estimate linkage stability across relevant groups. The methods used in establishing the overall link must be applied separately for each relevant group. The variation in the results for different groups at each score level can be computed and then averaged across score levels to estimate overall linkage stability. (In doing so, it may be useful to weight the different score levels in proportion to the number of examinees in the different groups at each level.) If linear projection is used, then standard statistical techniques like analysis of covariance can be used to estimate the extent to which regression slopes and intercepts are constant across different groups of students within linkage.

Anchor Test Designs

Sometimes it is not feasible to administer two tests in their entirety to a single group of students. Anchor test designs are commonly used in equating studies, but they cause significant difficulties in developing and evaluating linkages. It is not possible with this design, for example, to correlate the two tests directly. The best that can be done is to examine the similarity of the correlations of each test with the anchor. Moreover, additional variation may be introduced in assessing linkage stability across relevant groups as the groups could differ in significant ways on the anchor test even if they do not differ on the two tests being linked.

Additional Data Collections

It may or may not be possible to include sufficient numbers of examinees from all relevant groups in the initial linkage development data collection. Even when it is, one or more additional data collections will be required to establish the stability of a linkage over time. A number of more or less subtle changes, from changes in instruction to changes in cohort characteristics, may affect a linkage, leading to changes in the extent to which one test is relatively easier or harder than another for specific groups of students. Linkages that look good at first often fail to hold up over even short periods of time, as shown in the North Carolina and Kentucky studies mentioned above (Williams et al., 1995; Koretz, 1998). If a linkage is to be used beyond the initial development sample, some effort should be made to assess the stability of the linkage over time. The design issues and analysis procedures outlined above also apply to follow-up data collections.

ONE FINAL CAUTION

Error in the formation of linkages between tests can remain hidden from immediate view unless serious efforts are made to ferret them out. Statistical procedures can be applied to data that look reasonable and that pass various checks on their quality to ensure that there are no hidden errors. Even if two tests appear to measure similar things to content experts and "pass" a careful statistical evaluation, it is important to explicitly examine the stability of a linkage across the important subgroups of test takers and to check its stability over time.

3

Challenges of Linking to NAEP

In recent years there has been increasing interest in linkage to the National Assessment of Educational Progress (NAEP). A survey of NAEP's constituents asked respondents to assess their state's willingness to pay for three different services: a state-level assessment using NAEP's current approach; linking NAEP results with the state's regular assessment; and the provision of extra "NAEP-like" assessments for states to use as they wish. Although states were unwilling to pay for most services, two-thirds said they would pay to develop linkages between their state assessments and NAEP (Levine et al., 1998). Several states have already begun partial linkages: three states compare one component of their assessment program to NAEP; two link at least one component of their state results to the NAEP results; and one links at least one component of its assessment to the NAEP scale (Bond et al., 1998). In addition, the Voluntary National Tests are being designed to be linked to NAEP.

The appeal of being able to link tests to NAEP is not hard to understand. Doing so would enhance substantially the utility of NAEP information. Currently, NAEP reports results at the national and state levels only and thus provides limited information about the quality of schooling within a state. By linking other results to NAEP, educators and policy makers would be able to compare student, school, and district results to statewide, regional, and national results and so would have a better understanding of how their students and schools are performing and what the national results mean for local decision makers. Moreover, by using the NAEP achievement levels, parents, educators, and policy makers would have more information about how students perform in relation to national benchmarks for achievement.

Linking state assessments to NAEP would also enable states to evaluate their own assessments against a national criterion and to compare assessments with those of other states, using NAEP as the common denominator. And a NAEP link would permit associations with other national databases, such as the Common Core of Data and the Schools and Staffing Survey, which would enhance the quality of information available about school factors associated with achievement (Wu et al., 1997).

While the prospect of linking state tests to NAEP has substantial appeal, some have raised concern that doing so might undermine the quality of NAEP (e.g., Hill, 1998). The closer NAEP comes to local tests, the less it looks like an independent barometer of student achievement with low stakes for students or schools. Moreover, the possibility of linking state and commercial tests to NAEP poses serious challenges, even greater than those present in linking other tests. To understand these unique challenges, it is first necessary to understand the distinct character of NAEP.

DISTINCT CHARACTER OF NAEP

NAEP is a periodically administered, federally sponsored survey of a nationally representative sample of U.S. students that assesses student achievement in key subjects. It combines the data from all test takers and uses the resulting aggregate information to monitor and report on the academic performance of U.S. children as a group, as well as by specific subgroups of the student population. NAEP was not designed to provide achievement information about individual students. Rather, NAEP reports the aggregate, or collective, performance of students and it does so in two ways—scale scores and achievement levels: scale scores provide information about the distribution of student achievement for groups and subgroups in terms of a continuous scale; achievement levels are used to characterize student achievement as basic, proficient, or advanced, using ranges of performance established for each grade. The National Assessment Governing Board (NAGB), the body that governs the NAEP program, provides definitions for the three achievement levels. Student achievement that falls below the basic range is categorized as below basic (U.S. Department of Education, 1997).

NAEP uses matrix sampling to achieve two goals. First, students are asked to answer a relatively small number of test questions, so that the testing task given to students takes a relatively short time. Second, by asking different sets of questions of different students, the assessments cover a much larger array of questions than those given to any one student. By carefully balancing the sets of questions, called blocks, so that each block is taken by the same number of students, an equal number of students is presented with each item, making it possible to estimate the distribution of student scores by pooling data across test takers (Mislevy et al., 1992; Beaton and Gonzalez, 1995). The price paid for this flexibility is the inability of these assessments to collect enough data from any single student to provide valid individual scores.

NAEP's structure is unique: each student in the NAEP national sample takes only one booklet that contains a few short blocks of NAEP items in a single subject area (generally, three 15-minute or two 25-minute blocks), and no student's test booklet is fully representative of the entire NAEP assessment in that subject area. The scores for the item blocks a student takes are used to predict his or her performance on the entire assessment. Thus, the portion of NAEP any one student takes is unlikely to be comparable in content to the full knowledge domain covered by an individual test taker in a state or commercial test (see, e.g., U.S. Department of Education, 1997; National Research Council, 1996; Beaton and Gonzalez, 1995; U.S. Congress, Office of Technology Assessment, 1992). These characteristics of NAEP greatly increase the difficulty of establishing valid and reliable links between commercial and state tests and NAEP.

However, a matrix sampling design does not pose a permanently insuperable barrier to linking. One could design a linking experiment in which students in a nationally representative sample take a long form of NAEP containing, say, six blocks of test items rather than the typical two or three blocks, as well as a test that was to be linked to NAEP. If a student is assessed with six blocks of NAEP items, it is likely that his or her location on the NAEP scale and his or her assignment to a NAEP achievement-level category will be estimated with reasonable precision. If the test to be equated to NAEP and the conditions of administration and use of the test are sufficiently similar to those of NAEP, a student's score on the linked test likely might then be used to estimate his or her NAEP achievement-level placement with acceptable precision.

LINKING TO NAEP

A number of studies have attempted to link tests or test batteries to NAEP (see Table 2-1). To do so, they have administered several blocks of NAEP items as a substitute for a NAEP test to individual students and scored them using NAEP methods. In effect, the scores are weighted averages of the item scores, but the item weights depend on the characteristics of the item and on the pattern of item responses given by the individual. Recent proposals to create a NAEP test for use in linking (see, e.g., Yen, 1998) have not yet been realized.

Test results can be linked to NAEP scores at different levels of aggregation, and several studies have done so. However, when an assessment is only modestly related to the NAEP scale, links to enable comparing aggregate results, such as averages for states or school districts, would be different from links designed for reporting individual results. The inevitable consequence of this difference is that the proportions of students with scores predicted to be in each of the proficiency categories would depend on which link was used. Individual scores are generally linked to NAEP with the projection method, which is based on regression. Using regression improperly to carry out a projection-based linkage for individuals could result in many fewer students with projected scores in the "advanced" range and also fewer in the "below basic" range. Although the regression approach makes statistical sense, it raises problems if the results are intended to be used for policy purposes.

Linking Large-Scale Assessments

Many studies have compared the aggregate NAEP results with similar results from state-level assessments, from international assessments, or from other testing programs (see e.g., National Center for Education Statistics, 1998; Pashley and Phillips, 1993; Linn and Kiplinger, 1995). These studies were designed to compare populations of students. For example, the Armed Services Vocational Aptitude Battery (ASVAB), the set of tests used for entrance in to the U.S. Armed Services, has been compared with the NAEP results in 12th-grade mathematics. A link between the ASVAB and NAEP proficiencies was obtained by projecting ASVAB scores to the NAEP scale. The Armed Services could thus compare the achievement of their recruits with all U.S. students.

Studies comparing populations on the NAEP and another assessment must be done with great care because the tests being linked seldom have the same format or content. The usual method of checking on the validity of the link has been to closely compare the content and format and to compare the results of linking with different subgroups. The ASVAB mathematics tests do not cover some aspects of mathematics that are in the NAEP assessment, especially geometry. However, the ASVAB link was constructed by projecting to the NAEP scale from a combination of all 10 subtests of the ASVAB, and some of the mechanical comprehension tests were judged to represent geometry concepts to some degree. Statistical checks were made by constructing separate links for low-scoring and high-scoring examinees. Both links provided very comparable results. A comparison of the link from ASVAB to NAEP showed very small differences.[1] However, doubt was cast on the validity of the link because it suggested a much lower standing of the military recruits on the NAEP scale than was indicated by norms for the ASVAB based on the full population of youth between 17 and 23 years of age. This large difference suggested to the researchers that the motivation of their recruits in the study was not high, probably since they knew that the test scores would not have any consequences for them (Bloxom et al., 1995).

The second International Assessment of Educational Progress (IAEP) in science and mathematics was linked to NAEP in order to compare international achievement in terms of NAEP proficiency standards. In fact, two different links were developed. First, the IAEP distribution of achievement for the United States was compared with the NAEP 1992 distribution and aligned using statistical moderation (Beaton and Gonzales, 1993). Second, projection was used with a sample of students participating in the 1992 NAEP who also took the IEAP (Pashley and Phillips, 1993). The resulting projection of the IAEP scale to the NAEP scale could be checked by comparing actual NAEP results for the United States as a whole with the predictions of NAEP results from the IAEP results of the U.S. sample that had taken the IAEP. The differences of proportions of students' achieving at basic or above, proficient or above, and advanced, ranged from 0.01 to 0.03, corresponding to differences of from 0.01 to 0.10 standard deviations on the NAEP scale. Given the differences in the assessments, the link was very close.

---

[1] In terms of effect sizes, which statisticians use to describe the meaning of observed numerical differences (see, e.g., Mosteller, 1995) the ASVAB-NAEP link was very close, 0.02 standard deviations.

The Third International Mathematics and Science Study (TIMSS) was linked to NAEP by statistical moderation, because there was insufficient funding to do a same-group study (National Center for Education Statistics, 1998). The results could be checked by using data from the state of Minnesota, which had participated as a unit in TIMSS, for 8th-grade mathematics and science. The NAEP performance of Minnesota students in mathematics, when linked with TIMSS, predicted that 6 percent of Minnesota students would place among the top 10 percent internationally; 7 percent scored at that level on the actual TIMSS. Also, 62 percent were predicted by the link to score in the top half of the international sample; in fact, 57 percent scored in the top half internationally. The NAEP-TIMSS link for the 8th-grade science assessment indicated that 16 percent of the students would be classified in the top 10 percent internationally, based on NAEP results; on the actual TIMSS, 20 percent of the students scored at that level. In science, NAEP results predicted that 69 percent of Minnesota students would be among the top half of the international distribution; 67 percent actually scored in the top half. These close matches are encouraging. Data from other states and other grades have not yet been reported.

Linking Commercial and State Tests

The earliest studies linking commercial and state assessments to the NAEP scale examined the efficacy of simple distribution-matching procedures for this purpose. Ercikan (1997) reported obtaining statistical links of the 8th-grade mathematics scale of the California Achievement Test (CAT) in four states by comparing the test results to the state's student performance on the NAEP trial state assessment. The four states used slightly different versions of the CAT, all of which were calibrated to a common scale by the publisher. The four links to NAEP had substantial differences. One way to express the differences is to note that the same score of 56 on the CAT scale, a score at about the average for 8th graders, would have translated to NAEP scale scores of 254, 260, 268, and 274, depending on the state.[2] Another way to express the differences is to note that a score that appeared to be as good as 50 percent of the national

---

[2]The NAEP score scale has a standard deviation, within grade, of about 30 to 35, so the smallest difference is about 0.18 standard deviation, and the largest difference is about 0.6 standard deviation.

student population, judging from the link observed in one state, would seem to be as good 57 percent to 72 percent of the national student population, using linkages from the other states. Links with this kind of discrepancy pose serious problems of interpretability.

A distribution-matching method was also used by Linn and Kiplinger (1995) to link the NAEP results for 8th-grade mathematics with results on the Stanford Achievement Test in two states. In each state, the researchers then compared results based on obtaining separate links for males and females. The results showed virtually no difference in the linked scales at the upper end of the score range, but at the lower range, the difference was about 10 points on the NAEP scale, or about 0.3 standard deviation. The same low score (of 30) on the commercial test would translate into a considerably lower NAEP equivalent for a girl than for a boy. These authors also examined linkage consistency of state-NAEP links in four states across two years. They found differences of from 0.0 to 0.15 standard deviation between 1990 and 1992. Such differences might be considered small in some contexts, but they are disturbing when assessing national student accomplishments.

These two studies show that distribution-matching methods are not well suited to this task. When a distribution-matching method is used to equate two tests, the tests should have the same format and content. Moreover, the groups taking the two tests should be formed by random assignment from a single population, and the tests should be given at the same time under the same conditions. In neither study was the content of the state assessment a close match with the NAEP content, and in neither study did the distributions represent the same population. In both cases, although the state assessment was intended to be given to every student, exceptions were sometimes made for students with physical or learning disabilities, and the testing was done at different times, in different ways.

A much more specialized kind of equipercentile equating was developed in the early 1990s between the Kentucky Instructional Results Information System (KIRIS) and the NAEP achievement-level categories (Kentucky Department of Education, 1995). The results showed a modest relationship between achievement on the two tests. Because the results from KIRIS are reported only on a four-category scale—students are labeled novice, apprentice, proficient, or distinguished—this linkage was unusual in that it did not translate numerical scores on the statewide scale into numerical scores on the NAEP scale. Instead, it sought cut-points on the NAEP scale that gave results matching those obtained with KIRIS.[3]

The early, relatively disappointing, results using distribution-matching methods led subsequent researchers to attempt to use projection when linking statewide assessments to the NAEP scale. Projection can include terms to account for possible variation in the relationship between the state assessments and the NAEP scale for various subpopulations. Including such group-level terms implies a corresponding change in the goals of the linkage. A projection that uses different relationships between two tests for different subgroups or under different "conditions" (an aspect of the procedure often referred to as "conditioning") is designed to produce accurate predictions of aggregated score distributions; it is generally not used to produce individual scores.

The North Carolina Department of Public Instruction linked mathematics on its comprehensive academic testing program with the NAEP scale (Williams et al., 1995). The state's end-of-grade tests were closely aligned with the state curriculum, but not with NAEP, so content alignment was not close. Nevertheless, a study was done linking the North Carolina 8th-grade end-of-grade test in mathematics with the NAEP 8th-grade mathematics assessment. A representative sample of students took a short form of the end-of-grade test and a short form of the NAEP mathematics assessment, consisting of two blocks of related items. There was no requirement that individual scores be linked; the main objective was inference about the score distribution for the state in years when NAEP was not administered. This linkage used projection, involving a statistical regression of NAEP scores on the state assessment scores. For the analysis, scores on the NAEP blocks were determined from the student responses, using the NAEP item parameters in the framework of item response theory, but not including the elaborate conditioning analysis used by NAEP. The regular scores of these students on the North Carolina assessment were used. A satisfactory linking was obtained, which permitted statewide statistics on the NAEP scale (such as the mean, or the quartiles usually reported) to be predicted with only modest

---

[3]If the linkage had been at the level of the test scores, the relatively modest relationship between NAEP and KIRIS achievement estimates would have given pause. It was possible to estimate correlations between the average scores for schools on the NAEP and KIRIS scales; for mathematics, those correlations were .74, .78, and .79 for grades 4, 8, and 12, respectively. Those correlations are considerably lower than are usually obtained between two equated tests.

statistical standard error bands. However, separate links for two ethnic groups showed differences of about 0.28 standard deviation. Some of the effect may be an artifact of the use of regression in developing the links. The practical difference would be between the link for the separate groups and the link for the combined group: taking those factors into consideration leaves a difference of at least 0.1 to 0.2 standard deviation on average, which could result in misleading interpretations of results.

Links for Individual Proficiencies

A recent study linked individual scores on assessments in four separate states to the 1996 NAEP mathematics assessment for both 4th and 8th grades (McLaughlin, 1998). Alignment of the content of the state assessments with the NAEP mathematics framework was better in some states than in others. In each case, scores of individual students in the NAEP sample in that state were compared with their scores on the state mathematics assessment. The objectives of each state were somewhat narrower than the full NAEP framework. The results differ by states in detail, but are similar in many respects. The link was slightly better for grade 8 than for grade 4. McLaughlin (1998:43) summarizes the results as follows:

> NAEP measurement error, which has a standard deviation of 9 or 10, except in State #1 (where it is 12.5), is not affected by the accuracy of the linkage. However, the prediction error, which is attributable to the linkage, has a standard deviation that ranges from 16 to 20. The sum of the two sources of error variance yield an estimate of the expected error in individually predicted NAEP plausible values, a standard deviation of 18 to 22 points on the NAEP scale. Thus, a 95 percent confidence interval would range across more than 70 points on the NAEP scale. Clearly the linkage does not support reporting individual NAEP scores based on state assessment information, no matter how reliable the state assessment.

The negative result is not unexpected. Using actual NAEP results is a slim reed because each person takes such a short test. When the unreliability of NAEP results for individuals is coupled with differences between NAEP and state assessments and differences in the administration conditions, the resulting links cannot be expected to yield precise links. These threats to linkage cannot be overcome by simply using the same test takers on both assessments.[4]

---

[4]It is important to keep the magnitude of this problem in the proper perspective, i.e., by comparing the degree of spread of the confidence interval after the linkage with the

CHALLENGES TO THE VALIDITY OF LINKAGE TO NAEP

As discussed in Chapter 2, a number of features of tests, as well as the purposes and conditions of their use, influence the likelihood that valid links can be established. These features apply with equal force to the linking of any test to NAEP and to the interpretation of a student's scores on any test, including the proposed Voluntary National Tests, in terms of the NAEP scale or the NAEP achievement levels. The unique character of NAEP, which makes it unlike most state and commercial tests in design and implementation, poses significant challenges to linkage.

Unique Characteristics of NAEP

Content Coverage

NAEP's distinctive characteristics present special challenges of content comparability with other tests (see, e.g., Kenney and Silver, 1997). NAEP content is determined through a rigorous and lengthy consensus process that culminates in "frameworks" deemed relevant to NAEP's principal goal of monitoring aggregate student performance for the nation as a whole. NAEP content is not supposed to reflect particular state or local curricular goals, but rather a broad national consensus on what is or should be taught; by design, its content is different from that of many state assessments (Campbell et al., 1994).

Item Format Distribution

Like its content, the format of the NAEP assessment is derived through a national consensus process and is unlikely to match precisely the format of particular state or commercial tests. The proposed format distribution of the Voluntary National Tests, for example, is 80 percent multiple-choice items and 20 percent constructed-response items, compared with the approximately 50-50 distribution of NAEP items across these format categories.

The mix of item formats on a test makes an enormous difference in

---

size of the confidence interval before the linkage. In McLaughlin's study this comparison was not possible. The Pashley and Phillips study (1993) comes closer to permitting this kind of comparison.

relative performance, particularly with the use of achievement levels. As Linn et al. (1992) have shown, the distribution of students assigned to the NAEP achievement levels varies dramatically when those who establish NAEP achievement levels consider selected-response (e.g., multiple-choice) and extended-response test items. In the most extreme case, for one subject in the 1990 NAEP Trial State Assessment, 78 percent of examinees would have been placed in the "basic" achievement level or higher on the basis of the selected-response NAEP items, while only 3 percent would have been so placed on the basis of the extended-response NAEP items. Although corresponding differences were less extreme for other NAEP assessments, they were substantial. These findings suggest that the problem of congruence between the abilities and knowledge suggested by students' performances on the items of a linked test and the abilities and knowledge described by the NAEP achievement levels will be exacerbated to the extent that the item format distribution of a linked test differs markedly from that of NAEP.

Test Administration

As a national survey designed to monitor overall educational performance, NAEP is administered in different ways than many state and commercial tests. As a result, the conditions of test administration—from the time of year in which the test is administered to who (the classroom teacher or an external administrator) administers it—are likely to differ between state tests and NAEP. Such differences in test administration can affect test results and so could affect any links between NAEP and other tests.

Test Use

Because it does not currently produce individual student scores, NAEP is the prime example of a low-stakes test—one on which few consequences are associated with performance. As a result, teachers have little incentive to prepare students to perform well on NAEP, and students have little motivation to perform at their best (see, e.g., O'Neil et al., 1992; Kiplinger and Linn, 1996). State tests, in contrast, often have serious consequences associated with the results, and teachers and students place great emphasis on improving performance. This difference could significantly threaten the quality of a link between a state test and NAEP.

Moreover, the difference between the stakes attached to state tests and NAEP threaten the stability and robustness of linkages over time. Since state curriculum frameworks, adopted state curricula, and accountability pressures are likely to encourage teachers to teach to the state accountability test (or insist that they do so) and no such pressures exist for NAEP, a linkage between a high-stakes test and NAEP is unlikely to be robust over time. Students' improvements over time on a high-stakes statewide test are unlikely to be mirrored by commensurate gains on NAEP unless the statewide accountability test is congruent to its counterpart NAEP assessment in terms of content, format, and skill demands.

Linking to NAEP Achievement Levels

In addition to the challenges posed for linking presented by the unique features of NAEP's design, the use of NAEP achievement levels as a way of reporting results from a linked test pose other challenges. The NAEP achievement levels have been the subject of substantial discussion and controversy (Stufflebeam et al., 1991; Linn et al., 1991; Shepard et al., 1993; U.S. General Accounting Office, 1993; Cizek, 1993; Kane, 1993; National Research Council, 1999b). We do not engage that issue here, but we note that linking tests to NAEP for the purpose of categorizing individual students with respect to the NAEP achievement levels is a use that has not yet been considered: this use gives rise to novel opportunities as well as novel problems.

The NAEP achievement levels carry labels—"basic," "proficient," and "advanced"—as well as paragraphs that describe the knowledge, skills, and abilities of students whose NAEP performance warrants assignment to those levels. These paragraphs, called achievement-level descriptors, represent subsets of the achievement domain that a NAEP assessment measures, which have presumably been mastered by students who are classified into the named achievement level.

Use of linking to place individual students into NAEP achievement levels would provide an opportunity to demonstrate the validity of the NAEP achievement-level descriptors, as well as potential evidence of their validity or invalidity. Since the classification of individual students into NAEP achievement levels has not been done, there has been no public opportunity to compare the performances of individual students on NAEP items and the descriptions of their knowledge, skills, and abilities provided by the NAEP achievement levels. A public report of the detailed results of a linking study would provide such an opportunity. In addition, the validity of the placement of individual students into NAEP achievement-level categories on the basis of their performances on a linked test could also be assessed. Again, a public report of the detailed results of a linking study would permit comparison of the performance of individual students on the linked test and the descriptions of their knowledge, skills, and abilities provided by the NAEP achievement levels. Such comparisons would provide direct evidence of the validity of important inferences that the linkage would claim to support. We do not know of any plans for such a study at this time.

4

Tests and Testing in the United States: A Picture of Diversity

In Chapter 2 we examine the factors that must be considered in determining the validity of linkage. In this chapter we examine the way these factors are reflected in tests in the United States and in the potential impact on attempts to link tests.

Educational testing in the United States is a diverse and complex enterprise. This diversity reflects both the current availability of a vast array of instruments to measure student achievement and the American decentralized system of educational governance, which allows officials in 50 states and approximately 15,000 school districts to choose what tests will be used in their jurisdictions. Thirty years ago, assessment of student achievement was synonymous with norm-referenced testing and an almost exclusive reliance on multiple-choice measures that ranked students, schools, and states in comparison with one another (McDonnell, 1994). Now, educators and policy makers are able to select from a variety of tests based on local educational needs and local decisions about what students should know and be able to do, as well as beliefs about the nature of accountability for students, teachers, and schools.

The diversity in educational testing has increased as states and districts have moved rapidly to revise their curricular goals, to reflect high expectations for student learning, and have adopted or created new instruments to measure student performance that are aligned with those goals.

The diversity of tests and testing programs can be characterized on three dimensions: (1) test type, or the kind of instrument used to assess performance; (2) test content, or the skills and knowledge measured by a particular test; and (3) the purposes for testing and selecting specific instruments.

In this chapter we examine these three dimensions in the context of linking. It is important to note that we focus here on large-scale assessments, which are used by states, districts, and the nation to measure the achievement of large groups of students. Teacher-made classroom assessments and school- and district-developed assessments, while important tools for instruction and program planning, are beyond the scope of our discussion.

TYPES OF TESTS

Item Format

Many different item and task formats are used in assessments of student achievement, and the effect of format differences on linkages can be substantial. Selected-response items, such as multiple-choice questions, require test takers to select the one best answer from a set of alternatives and to mark the answer on a separate answer sheet or directly on a test paper. Constructed-response items require the test taker to answer questions without being provided alternatives from which to select the correct response. Constructed-response items include short-answer format items that may require a test taker to fill in a blank or to answer a question by writing a short response on the test paper or an answer sheet (e.g., $13 + 28 =$ ____). A longer constructed-response item may require test takers to make simple lists; to write one or two sentences, a paragraph, or an extended essay; or to solve multiple-step mathematics problems and explain how they arrived at their solutions. (These latter two examples can also be considered performance tasks.)

Students who have not had experience with different item types may perform poorly on unfamiliar formats not because they do not know the material, but because they do not know how to devise responses. As a consequence, students who have little or no experience with answering long constructed-response items may simply omit them on a test, thereby producing a misleadingly low score. If a test that requires students to answer questions posed in an unfamiliar or difficult format is linked to a test with a more familiar format, it could be difficult to determine whether the relationship between the two linked tests is a result of test format differences or a valid comparison of student achievement.

There are other issues and cautions regarding attempts to link different assessments that contain different item types. In writing, for example, different item types measure writing ability in different ways. Selected-response items that measure vocabulary, grammar, writing mechanics, and editing skills might positively correlate with performance on an item requiring a constructed-response items that measures the quality of student prose. But who would assert that an extensive vocabulary, proper use of grammar, capitalization, punctuation, and good editing skills are the same as the creative process of writing? It is likely that using a statistical linking procedure to predict expected performance on a performance-based writing assessment from the results obtained from selected-response items (and vice versa) could provide inappropriate and misleading information.

Scoring

Different types of items require different scoring methods. Selected-response items are generally scored by machine. Examinees fill in a "box" or "bubble" indicating their answers, and the answer form is scanned into a computer, which also contains the answer key that specifies the response options that are correct. There is only one right answer, and the response is marked as "right" or "wrong." This type of scoring is relatively inexpensive and is highly reliable.

Constructed-response items must be scored by expert judges or raters, using specified scoring guides or rubrics. The reliability of the scoring process depends on such factors as the specificity of the scoring rubric, the rater's level of expertise, the quality of the training provided to the raters, and the extent of monitoring of interrater reliability throughout the scoring process. If any of these factors varies significantly, test reliability will be affected and measurement errors will be introduced (Herman, 1997). For example, several studies have demonstrated the differential effects of students' handwriting on raters' scoring of constructed-response answers on tests (see, e.g., Breland et al., 1994) This differential scoring affected the reliability of the grades assigned to some constructed-response items. Linking tests with different measurement error (reliability) could produce different linked results for each administration of the tests. In the diverse and complex landscape of testing, it is not uncommon to find variation in scoring practices among states. Scoring is a major concern in linking tests containing constructed-response items.

Increasingly, both "off-the-shelf" commercial tests and tests customized to consumer specifications are being constructed as mixed-model assessments that contain items of different types in varying proportions. The mix of item formats on a test makes a difference in student performance (see, e.g., Shavelson et al., 1992; Wester, 1995; Yen and Ferrara, 1997). Two tests of the same subject domain but containing a different mix of item formats may not be comparable in terms of difficulty and may not be equally reliable. Thus, linking tests that are not similar in format may challenge the ability to draw valid inferences from the linked results.

Norm-Referenced and Criterion-Referenced Test Interpretations

Although it is common practice to do so, labeling assessment instruments as norm-referenced or criterion-referenced is somewhat misleading (see, e.g., Cronbach, 1984; Glaser, 1963; Messick, 1989; Feldt and Brennan, 1989). It is the interpretation of the resulting scores that is norm-referenced or criterion-referenced, not the test instrument itself. In fact, raw scores, the exact count or measure of how many items a test taker answered correctly, can be interpreted within both norm-referenced and criterion-referenced frameworks.

Norm-referenced interpretations provide a means for comparing a student's achievement with that of others, determining how a student ranks in comparison with a sample of students, or norm group. When test developers create a new test or a new version of a test, they first administer it to a sample of students across the nation; this sample becomes the norm group. The composition of this sample varies by publisher, test, and the publisher's beliefs about what constitutes an appropriate sample.

The composition of a norm group has an effect on the validity of the inferences that can be drawn from the results and, hence, on the validity of any inferences drawn from comparisons between results on different tests (Peterson et al., 1993). For example, percentile rank, a term that expresses what part of the norm group earned scores that fell below the test taker's score, must always be interpreted with reference to the group from which they were derived (Cronbach, 1984). One norm group could be composed of relatively high-performing students, and a student taking a test normed against that group would have to perform very well in order to end up in a high percentile ranking. In contrast, a student taking a test normed against relatively poor performers would not have to perform as well in order to achieve a high percentile ranking. Therefore, if two students taking different tests normed on different groups both are in the 85th percentile on their respective tests, one has no way of knowing how well they performed in comparison with each other. While it is unlikely they performed equally well (because the norm groups differ), it is not possible to know with precision how much better one student performed than the other. Thus, linking scores from achievement tests that were normed on different groups will affect the validity of the inferences drawn from the link.

Examples of nationally normed achievement tests currently used by many states and school districts include the Iowa Tests of Basic Skills (ITBS), published by Riverside Publishing Company; the Stanford Achievement Test-Ninth Edition (SAT-9), published by Harcourt Brace Educational Measurement; and TerraNova, published by CTB/McGraw-Hill. Although these commercially developed achievement tests appear on the surface to be similar (see Chapter 2), they are, in fact, quite different in frameworks, content emphasis, item difficulty, and item sampling techniques, and they are normed on different populations. These differences may reflect the publishers' efforts to capture specialized markets and meet state and local demands for tests with particular features (see, e.g., Yen, 1998), or they may be the result of historical differences in test development. School officials and policy makers often choose a particular test because of the ways in which it differs from other, similar tests. However, the degree to which tests differ will affect the validity of any links between them.

Criterion-referenced interpretations indicate the student's level of performance relative to a criterion, or standard of performance, rather than relative to other students' performance. This interpretation is based on descriptions or standards of what students should know and be able to do, with performance being gauged against the established standard. Frequently, the meaning is given in terms of a cutscore: students who score above a certain point are considered to have mastered the material, and those who score below it are considered to have not fully met the standard. Established levels of mastery on state assessments vary from test to test and application to application, even when tests purport to measure the same content domain. This variation further complicates linkage.

An analogy that is often used to illustrate the difference between norm-referenced and criterion-referenced interpretations is mountain climbing. Norm-referenced interpretations can tell where the members of the climbing party are relative to each other—who is in the lead, who is in the middle, and who is lagging behind; however, they cannot tell you the location of the climbing party on the mountain. For example, the leaders might be less than half-way up the mountain or at the peak, and norm-referenced interpretations cannot distinguish between the two possibilities. A criterion-referenced interpretation, however, can tell you which of the climbers has achieved the target level of performance, say, the summit, and which are the less proficient climbers who need more instruction, training, or equipment. But note that neither kind of measure can tell you how high the mountain is or how the climber is performing relative to other climbers who are climbing other mountains in other places; this kind of analysis requires linking.

Tests that provide norm-referenced interpretations are designed to produce a range of scores, in order to show how students rank against their peers and against the norm group. To maximize the reliability of a percentile ranking within a group, test developers try to create a test that is able to generate scores from near zero to the highest possible score. To accomplish this, test developers include a few items that are so easy that virtually all of the test takers will get them correct and a few items that are so difficult that only the highest achievers can answer them correctly. The majority of the items, however, are of medium difficulty. In contrast, developers of standards-based assessments do not focus as much on generating scores that represent the full range of possible scores: rather, they try to include items that measure the full range of knowledge and skills necessary to demonstrate mastery of a concept. Standards-based assessments and other measures designed to provide criterion-referenced interpretations incorporate specified performance goals that are set by educators or policy makers in accordance with beliefs about what constitutes adequate performance. Their designers select items that will help to identify to what degree students have mastered the skills being assessed. These tests may be more difficult on some dimensions and easier on others than the tests designed for norm-referenced interpretations. Attempts to link tests with markedly different levels or ranges of difficulty may challenge the validity of the inferences that can be drawn from the linkage.

Test companies often claim that their tests can yield norm-referenced and criterion-referenced interpretations, which raises the possibility that two types of linkages could be established. The committee did not address this specific question in detail, but we note that in evaluating the quality of linkages one would not necessarily wish to adopt standards that exceed those that are applied to tests themselves.

TEST CONTENT

In addition to the variations in frameworks, content emphasis, item difficulty, and sampling techniques, tests vary significantly in their most fundamental aspect: the knowledge and skills they ask students to demonstrate. No test can possibly tap all the concepts and processes embodied in a subject area as vast as reading or mathematics. Instead, test makers construct a sample from the entire subject matter, called a domain. The samples that different test makers choose differ substantially. Thus, one can conclude that not only are the domains of reading and mathematics complex, but there are many subdomains and subsets of test elements (e.g., items) that can be used to measure them.

As discussed in Chapter 1, defining the domain is the first step in developing any test or assessment. The subject matter to be measured must be specified and distinguished from other, different subject matter. Distinctions among different domains are obvious. For example, reading, mathematics, and science are fundamentally different intellectual disciplines. The absolute nature of these distinctions begins to blur however, when one realizes that while the process of reading and the knowledge of science are certainly not the same thing, they overlap. Science knowledge is gained partly through reading, and effective reading enables students to gain science knowledge from a science text. Mathematics knowledge also is gained partly through reading, and science uses mathematics as a tool for scientific discovery. These overlaps among reading, mathematics, and science illustrate the challenges of defining any domain.

The diversity and variety in content domain sampling have implications for linking. Tests that measure different dimensions of a content domain must be viewed judiciously in any linkage project. When the content of two tests is the same, statistical linkage is possible; when the dimensions of content that have been sampled in two tests is not similar, limits on the inferences of linkage are substantial. Therefore, the content similarity of two tests is a high priority in evaluating and describing the linkage between them. In the next two sections we explore some dimensions of the domains of mathematics and reading to illustrate some of the issues involved in specifying a part of a domain for test purposes.

Mathematics

The domain of mathematics is very complex, and for all practical purposes mathematics curriculum and test developers must focus their efforts on only a part of the domain. That is, in defining a mathematics curriculum or developing a mathematics test, they must select topics from the whole domain of mathematics, based on a particular set of needs and purposes. For example, school mathematics—the mathematical concepts and processes relevant for kindergarten through high school (K-12)—can be thought of as one subdomain of the larger domain of mathematics. In addition, the various curricula taught in different school systems, and the various ways the schools choose to assess student mastery of content, are further subdomains of the subdomain of school mathematics.

A characterization of the subdomain of the K-12 school mathematics curriculum appears in *Curriculum and Evaluation Standards for School Mathematics* (hereafter, *Standards*) of the National Council of Teachers of Mathematics (NCTM) (1989). The *Standards* characterize the K-12 curriculum using three grade-level clusters that are roughly equivalent to the elementary (K-4), middle school (grades 5-8), and secondary (grades 9-12) levels, and it identifies four cognitive processes—problem solving, communication, reasoning, and connections—that cut across all grade levels; see Box 4-1 for a description. The *Standards* also define a number of widely recognized mathematical content topics (e.g., number and number relationships, algebra, statistics, geometry, measurement, and trigonometry), which are emphasized differently at different grade levels. For example, informal algebra topics, such as patterns, are introduced in the grade K-4 and grade 5-8 clusters, but a more formal treatment of algebra does not occur until the grade 9-12 cluster. To the extent test developers adhere to the *Standards*, their tests will share these emphases. However, while the NCTM *Standards* have been adopted widely by test publishers on a general level, at a specific level adherence to them may vary. Therefore, tests may vary in their mix of topics at particular grades.

BOX 4-1
Cognitive Processes of Math

Problem Solving. The process of mathematical problem solving is often characterized by the words of mathematician George Polya (1980:1) "To solve a problem is to find a way where no way is known offhand, to find a way out of difficulty, to find a way around an obstacle, to attain a desired end, that is not immediately attainable, by appropriate means." Problem solving is a method of inquiry and application that provides a context for learning and applying mathematics.

Communication. Communication as a mathematical process involves learning the signs, symbols, and terms of mathematics and thus has an important relationship to the disciplines of reading and writing. Students acquire the ability to communicate mathematically by reading, writing, and discussing mathematical concepts.

Reasoning. Mathematical reasoning involves making conjectures, gathering evidence, and building an argument. Reasoning is recognized by the mathematics education community as fundamental to knowing and doing mathematics.

Connections. There are two types of connections: connections between content areas such as geometry and algebra and connections between mathematics and other disciplines such as science, reading, and social studies. Within the K-12 mathematics curriculum, the *Standards* promote connections among the various content topics and between mathematics and these other disciplines.

SOURCE: National Council of Teachers of Mathematics (1989).

Reading

The skills that make up the domain of reading are characterized by *Standards for the English/Language Arts*, recently published by the National Council of Teachers of English (1996) as a joint project with the International Reading Association. Although the *Standards* and the processes of language and thinking that underlie them are inherently integrated in use and in teaching, reading tests tend to emphasize one of four dimensions in this domain: word recognition, passage comprehension, vocabulary, and reading inquiry. These dimensions are justifiable on the basis of the moderate to low correlations among them and fundamental differences in their psychological and educational meanings; see Box 4-2 for a description of these four dimensions.

BOX 4-2
Dimensions Emphasized in Reading Tests

Word Recognition. Initial reading acquisition is fundamentally a process of learning to recognize words. The cognitive, language, and neurological processes undergirding this process are not simple.

Passage Comprehension. Understanding the main idea of a passage is integral to reading. Comprehension of a paragraph may be measured by free recall, multiple-choice items, and short-answer questions. Passage comprehension depends on the ability to summarize, to use background knowledge to understand new information, to self-monitor the comprehension process, to know word meanings, and to build causal connections during reading. A wide array of complex cognitive processes is known to underlie passage comprehension (Kintsch, 1998; Lorch and Van den Broek, 1997; Pressley and Afflerbach, 1996). Many types of genres are used, including stories, poetry, exposition, and documents such as directions, to test possible comprehension.

Vocabulary. A traditional aspect of reading is word knowledge. Many assessments use multiple-choice formats to test students' knowledge of word meaning. Students may be asked to identify synonyms, antonyms, or definitions. Knowledge of individual word meanings is highly associated with passage comprehension, but word knowledge is not the same as understanding the main idea of a paragraph, and the moderate correlations between tests of vocabulary and comprehension reflect this relationship.

Reading Inquiry. Reading inquiry has been identified as a dimension of reading separable from passage comprehension. It involves cognitive strategies for judging relevance, locating important information, identifying information in different locations, and building a knowledge network from separate passages of text.

The diversity in defining and teaching the domain of reading and differences in emphases in curriculum and instructional methodology are reflected in the diversity of assessments that purport to measure the domain. Assessments of reading, like assessments of mathematics, vary in terms of the content, level of difficulty, and the cognitive skills tapped by the items selected for the test.

Sampling a Domain for Assessment

The domains of reading and mathematics are broad and heterogeneous. They both contain different components and dimensions. Any particular assessment of reading or mathematics taps a limited sample of the domain. No test asks all possible questions that could be asked. The content domain and sampling strategy for any given test are based on the purposes for assessment, the age of the students being tested, and beliefs about reading or mathematics processes.

States have different purposes for testing students and try to select tests that sample content domains appropriately for the intended use. Examples of two broad purposes that are directly affected by sampling are: obtaining student-level achievement information that can be used to report individual student progress and obtaining student-level achievement information to provide a picture of school-level achievement for accountability or for school improvement. Tests that yield norm-referenced interpretations are frequently used to obtain measures of individual student achievement. These tests are designed to distinguish among students as fully, quickly, and simply as possible. These criteria lead to using the fewest items and the fewest possible dimensions of the content domain while retaining high test reliability. The principle is to reduce the test to its minimum number of constructs and items while maximizing its ability to distinguish individual differences in achievement. For school accountability purposes, tests that yield criterion-referenced interpretations and include a broad array of constructs within the content domain are often used. Tests used effectively for accountability sample subdomains broadly, include cognitive processes needed across the domain, and require performance on complex tasks. The goal is to expand the number of constructs measured and, thus, taught. The test developer's aim is to maximize the scope of the assessment, rather than to minimize it. Linking the results from tests that sample a domain differently may lead to invalid inferences about student achievement and school performance.

TESTING IN STATES AND DISTRICTS

Trends in State Student Assessment Programs, published by the Council of Chief State School Officers (Bond et al., 1998), and *Quality Counts '98* (Education Week, 1998), published in collaboration with the Pew Charitable Trusts, indicate that nearly all states now have statewide assessment programs. These two reports indicate that states have made a major shift from off-the-shelf tests to state-developed criterion-referenced tests and customized tests that allow both norm-referenced and criterion-referenced interpretations. In different states, these assessments may stand alone, be given in conjunction with each other, or be paired with performance tasks, portfolio assessments, and writing samples.

Given the wide array of choices of test type, format, and content, officials in states and schools districts have much to choose from when designing testing programs; and they have chosen in many different ways (Table 4-1). These decisions are most often guided by the purposes for which the testing program is designed. In this section we discuss some of the decisions that policy makers and educators make in determining the scope and format of large-scale testing programs and the impact of these factors on linking.

State Approaches

In recent years, states have taken various approaches to meet ever-increasing demands for higher standards of student performance in academic content and skill areas. Current efforts focus on comprehensive systems of assessment that attempt to:

- incorporate content standards (statements of what students should know and be able to do);
- incorporate performance standards (descriptors of what kinds and levels of performance represent adequate learning);
- reflect curriculum and instruction designed to effectively deliver the knowledge and skills necessary for student learning and performance relative to content standards;
- determine the extent to which students have mastered the content and skills represented by the standards; and
- develop accountability indices that show how well students, schools, school districts, states, and other entities are demonstrating desirable levels of student achievement.

Purposes

It is safe to say that the ultimate purpose of assessment is to improve instruction and student learning. But many states differ in their relative emphasis on the use of assessments in program evaluation, curriculum planning, school performance reporting, and student diagnosis (Roeber et al., 1998), all of which are activities aimed at the ultimate goal of

TABLE 4-1 State Testing: A Snapshot of Diversity

State	Use of Commercial Tests	Use of Other Assessments
Alabama	Stanford Achievement Test 9, Otis Lennon School Ability Test	Alabama Kindergarten Assessment, Alabama Direct Assessment of Writing, Differential Aptitude Test, Basic Competency Test, Career Interest Inventory, End-of-Course Algebra and Geometry Test, Alabama High School Basic Skills Exit Exam
Alaska	California Achievement Test 5	
Arizona	Stanford Achievement Test 9	
Arkansas	Stanford Achievement Test 9	High School Proficiency Test
California	Stanford Achievement Test 9	Golden State Examinations
Colorado	Custom developed	CTB/McGraw-Hill item banks, NAEP items, and state items
Connecticut	Custom developed	Connecticut Mastery Test, Connecticut Academic Performance Test
Delaware	Custom developed	State-developed writing assessment
Florida	Custom developed	High School Competency Test, Florida Writing Assessment Program
Georgia	Iowa Tests of Basic Skills, Tests of Achievement Proficiency	Curriculum-Based Assessments, Georgia High School Graduation Tests, Georgia Kindergarten Assessment Program, Writing Assessment
Hawaii	Stanford Achievement Test 8	Hawaii State Test of Essential Competencies, Credit by Examination
Idaho	Iowa Tests of Basic Skills Form K, Tests of Achievement Proficiency	Direct Writing Assessment, Direct Mathematics Assessment
Illinois	Custom developed	Illinois Goals Assessment Program
Indiana	Custom developed	Indiana Statewide Testing for Educational Progress Plus
Iowa	No mandated statewide testing program, approximately 99 percent of all districts participate in the Iowa Tests of Basic Skills on a voluntary basis	

TABLE 4-1 (Continued)

State	Use of Commercial Tests	Use of Other Assessments
Kansas	Custom developed	Kansas Assessment Program (Kansas University Center for Educational Testing and Evaluation)
Kentucky	Custom developed	Kentucky Instructional Results Information System
Louisiana	California Achievement Test 5	Louisiana Educational Assessment Program
Maine	Custom developed	Maine Educational Assessment (Advanced Systems in Measurement, Inc.)
Maryland	Custom developed, Comprehensive Test of Basic Skills 5	Maryland Student Performance Assessment Program, Maryland Functional Tests, Maryland Writing Test
Massachusetts	Iowa Tests of Basic Skills, Iowa Tests of Educational Development	
Michigan	Custom developed	Michigan Educational Assessment Program: Criterion-referenced tests of 4th-, 7th-, and 11th-grade students in mathematics and reading and 5th-, 8th-, and 11th-grade students in science and writing; Michigan High School Proficiency Test
Minnesota	Custom developed	1996-1997 students took minimum competency literacy tests in reading and mathematics
Mississippi	Iowa Tests of Basic Skills, Tests of Achievement Proficiency	Functional Literacy Examination, Subject Area Testing Program
Missouri	Custom developed, TerraNova	Missouri Mastery and Achievement Test
Montana	Stanford Achievement Test, Iowa Tests of Basic Skills, Comprehensive Test of Basic Skills	
Nebraska	No statewide assessment program in 1996-1997	

TABLE 4-1 *(Continued)*

State	Use of Commercial Tests	Use of Other Assessments
Nevada	TerraNova	Grade 8 Writing Proficiency Exam, Grade 11 proficiency exam
New Hampshire	Custom developed	New Hampshire Education Improvement and Assessment Program (Advanced Systems in Measurement and Evaluation, Inc.)
New Jersey	Custom developed	Grade 11 High School Proficiency Test, Grade 8 Early Warning Test
New Mexico	Iowa Tests of Basic Skills, Form K	New Mexico High School Competency Exam, Portfolio Writing Assessment, Reading Assessment for Grades 1 and 2
New York	Custom developed	Occupational Education Proficiency Examinations, Preliminary Competency Tests, Program Evaluation Tests, Pupil Evaluation Program Tests, Regents Competency Tests, Regents Examination Program, Second Language Proficiency Examinations
North Carolina	Iowa Tests of Basic Skills	North Carolina End-of-Grade Tests
North Dakota	Comprehensive Test of Basic Skills/4, TCS	
Ohio	Custom developed	4th-, 6th-, 9th-, and 12th-Grade Proficiency Tests
Oklahoma	Iowa Tests of Basic Skills	Oklahoma Core Curriculum Tests
Oregon	Custom developed	Reading, Writing, and Mathematics Assessment
Pennsylvania	Custom developed	Writing, Reading, and Mathematics Assessment
Rhode Island	Metropolitan Achievement Test 7, Custom developed	Health Performance Assessment, Mathematics Performance Assessment, Writing Performance Assessment
South Carolina	Metropolitan Achievement Test 7, Custom developed	Basic Skills Assessment Program

TABLE 4-1 (Continued)

State	Use of Commercial Tests	Use of Other Assessments
South Dakota	Stanford Achievement Test 9, Metropolitan Achievement Test 7	
Tennessee	Custom developed	Tennessee Comprehensive Assessment Program (TCAP) Achievement Test Grades 2-8, TCAP Competency Graduation Test , TCAP Writing Assessment Grades 4, 8, and 11.
Texas	Custom developed	Texas Assessment of Academic Skills, Texas End-of-Course Tests
Utah	Stanford Achievement Test 9, Custom developed	Core Curriculum Assessment Program
Vermont	Has a voluntary state assessment program	New Standards Reference Exams in math, Portfolio assessment in math and writing
Virginia	Customized off the shelf	Literacy Passport Test, Degrees of Reading Power, Standards of Learning Assessments, Virginia State Assessment Program
Washington	Comprehensive Test of Basic Skills 4, Curriculum Frameworks Assessment System	
West Virginia	Comprehensive Test of Basic Skills	Writing Assessment, Metropolitan Readiness Test
Wisconsin	TerraNova, Custom developed	Knowledge and Concepts Tests, Wisconsin Reading Comprehension Test at Grade 3
Wyoming	State assessment program in vocational education only for students in grades 9-12	

NOTES: Custom-developed assessments result from a joint venture between a state and a commercial test publisher to design a test to the state's specification, perhaps to more closely match the state's curriculum than an off-the-shelf test. Customized off-the-shelf assessments result from modifications to a commercial test publisher's existing product.

SOURCE: Data from 1997 Council of Chief State School Officers Fall State Student Assessment Program Survey.

improved education; see Figures 4-1 and 4-2. More and more states are using (or are contemplating using) their assessment programs to make high-stakes decisions about people and programs, such as promoting students to the next grade, determining whether students will graduate from high school, grouping students for instructional purposes, making decisions about teacher tenure or bonuses, allocating resources to schools, or imposing sanctions on schools and districts (see, e.g., McLaughlin et al., 1995; McDonnell, 1997; National Research Council, 1999c).

Table 4-2 shows many of the varied uses of tests in the nation's schools today. Decisions about the purposes for testing will guide decisions about the content and format of selected tests; who should be tested and when; how results will be aggregated and reported; and who will be held accountable. Assessment programs that seek to guide instruction and those that seek to provide accountability may have significant differences in test design. When the same test is used for multiple purposes, the validity of the inference that can be drawn from the results may be jeopardized.

The committee realizes that information such as that in Tables 4-1 and 4-2 changes frequently and can be summarized differently in different reports. These tables are compiled from data collected by the Council of Chief State School Officer's Annual State Student Assessment Survey. The data are self-reported by the assessment director in the states' education departments and describe the assessment programs they operated during the 1996-1997 school year (Roeber et al., 1998). It is considered accurate at the time of reporting. These tables are included to show the choices states make in selecting assessment instruments and the diversity of purposes for the tests. They paint a clear picture that states' testing programs are diverse.

Population Tested

States make different determinations about who should be tested and how the testing should be conducted, especially with regard to students with disabilities or limited English-language proficiency. The movement toward educational accountability for all students is gaining momentum and is serving as an impetus for the inclusion of students with special needs who were formerly excluded from statewide assessments. In order to provide special needs students with access to assessments and an equal opportunity to demonstrate knowledge and skills, many states are offering

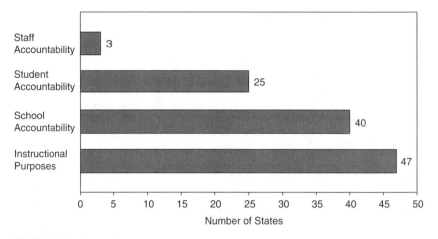

FIGURE 4-1 Types of assessment purposes.
SOURCE: Roeber et al. (1998).

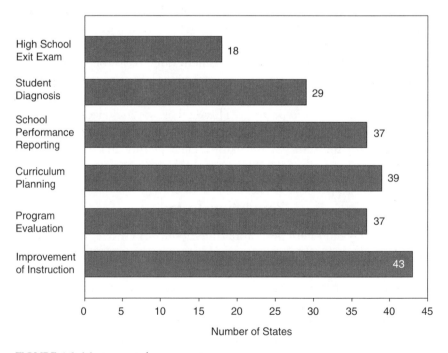

FIGURE 4-2 Most reported assessment purposes.
SOURCE: Roeber et al. (1998).

accommodations or modifications to their assessments. Currently, test accommodations are the most common response to the need to include more students in state assessments.

Test accommodations are changes made to test administration procedures in order to provide a student with access to the assessment and an equal opportunity to demonstrate knowledge and skills without affecting the reliability or validity of the assessment. That is, the accommodation should not change the test content, instructional level, performance criteria, or expectations for student performance. The purpose of accommodation is to remove variance that is not related to the domain of the test—that is, to level the playing field by eliminating irrelevant sources of differences in student performance. The most common test accommodations are changes in the timing or scheduling of the assessment; mode of presentation, such as Braille or large-print versions for the visually impaired or reading a writing assessment item to an auditory learner; or mode of responses, such as use of a scribe to record oral responses and fill in the test booklet. These approaches, when designed and implemented properly, provide scores that permit interpretations of student's knowledge or mastery of the domain without confounding the effects of their disability.

In the instances described above, those of accommodation, the *same* test is administered to all students, although the conditions in which the test is administered vary, which allows all students to participate. In contrast, a modification to an assessment changes the validity of the assessment since the test content, difficulty level, performance criteria, or expectations of the student may be different from that of the regular assessment. In a word, a different test is administered to some students. A common test modification is to read a reading assessment to an auditory learner. This changes what is measured: it is no longer an assessment of the ability to decode, comprehend, and use written information, but an assessment of the ability to decode, comprehend, and use oral information (see National Research Council, 1998).

In establishing linkages between different statewide assessment programs, it is important to ask how many students with disabilities or with limited English-language proficiency participate in a state's assessment programs, what kinds of accommodations and modifications are allowed that enable participation, and what scores are included in state reports of assessment results. One of the major considerations in linking two assessments is the comparability of the populations tested. For example, an

TABLE 4-2 Student Testing: Diversity of Purpose

State	Decisions for Students
Alabama	High school graduation
Alaska	
Arizona	
Arkansas	
California	Student diagnosis or placement
Colorado[a]	
Connecticut	Student diagnosis or placement
Delaware	
Florida	High school graduation
Georgia	High school graduation
Hawaii	High school graduation
Idaho	
Iowa[a]	
Illinois	
Indiana	
Kansas	
Kentucky	
Louisiana	Student promotion; high school graduation
Maine	Student diagnosis or placement
Maryland	High school graduation
Massachusetts	
Michigan	Student diagnosis or placement; endorsed diploma
Minnesota[a]	
Mississippi	High school graduation
Missouri	
Montana	

Decisions for Schools	Instructional Purposes
School performance reporting	Student diagnosis or placement; improve instruction; program evaluation
School performance reporting	Improve instruction
School performance reporting	Student diagnosis or placement; improve instruction; program evaluation
School performance reporting	Student diagnosis or placement; improve instruction; program evaluation
	Student diagnosis or placement
Awards or recognition; school performance reporting	Student diagnosis or placement; improve instruction; program evaluation
	Student diagnosis or placement; improve instruction; program evaluation
	Improve instruction; program evaluation
School performance reporting	Student diagnosis or placement; improve instruction; program evaluation
Awards or recognition; school performance reporting	Student diagnosis or placement; improve instruction; program evaluation
School performance reporting	Improve instruction
Accreditation	
Awards or recognition; school performance reporting; accreditation	Student diagnosis or placement; improve instruction; program evaluation
School performance reporting; accreditation	Student diagnosis or placement; improve instruction; program evaluation
Awards or recognition	Improve instruction; program evaluation
Awards or recognition; school performance reporting	Student diagnosis or placement; improve instruction; program evaluation
	Improve instruction; program evaluation
School performance reporting; skills guarantee; accreditation	Student diagnosis or placement; improve instruction; program evaluation
School performance reporting	Improve instruction
Awards or recognition; School performance reporting; accreditation	Improve instruction; program evaluation
School performance reporting; skills guarantee; accreditation	Student diagnosis or placement; improve instruction; program evaluation
School performance reporting; accreditation	Improve instruction; program evaluation
	Improve instruction; program evaluation

TABLE 4-2 (Continued)

State	Decisions for Students
Nebraska[a]	
Nevada	High school graduation
New Hampshire	
New Jersey	High school graduation
New Mexico	High school graduation
New York	Student diagnosis or placement; student promotion; honors diploma; endorsed diploma; high school graduation
North Carolina	Student diagnosis or placement; student promotion; high school graduation
North Dakota	Student diagnosis or placement
Ohio	High school graduation
Oklahoma	
Oregon	
Pennsylvania	
Rhode Island	
South Carolina	Student promotion; high school graduation
South Dakota	
Tennessee	Endorsed diploma; high school graduation
Texas	Student diagnosis or placement; high school graduation
Utah	Student diagnosis or placement
Vermont	
Virginia	Student diagnosis or placement; student ; promotion high school graduation
Washington	
West Virginia	
Wisconsin	
Wyoming	

[a]Colorado, Minnesota, and Nebraska did not administer any statewide assessments in 1995-1996. Iowa does not administer a statewide assessment.

Decisions for Schools	Instructional Purposes
School performance reporting; accreditation	Improve instruction; program evaluation
	Improve instruction; program evaluation
School performance reporting; accreditation	Student diagnosis or placement; improve instruction
School performance reporting; accreditation	Student diagnosis or placement; improve instruction; program evaluation
School performance reporting	Improve instruction; program evaluation
	Improve instruction; program evaluation
	Student diagnosis or placement; improve instruction; program evaluation
Awards or recognition; school performance reporting	Improve instruction; program evaluation
School performance reporting; accreditation	Student diagnosis or placement; improve instruction; program evaluation
School performance reporting	Improve instruction; program evaluation
School performance reporting	Student diagnosis or placement; program evaluation
School performance reporting	Improve instruction; program evaluation
Awards or recognition; school performance reporting; skills guarantee	Student diagnosis or placement; improve instruction; program evaluation
	Improve instruction; program evaluation
	Student diagnosis or placement; improve instruction; program evaluation
	Student diagnosis or placement; improve instruction; program evaluation
School performance reporting	Student diagnosis or placement; improve instruction; program evaluation
School performance reporting	Student diagnosis or placement; improve instruction; program evaluation
School performance reporting	Student diagnosis or placement; improve instruction; program evaluation
School performance reporting	Student diagnosis or placement; improve instruction; program evaluation
Skills guarantee; accreditation	Improve instruction
School performance reporting	Program evaluation
	Improve instruction; program evaluation

SOURCE: Data from 1996 Council of Chief State School Officers Fall State Student Assessment Program Survey.

attempt to link two assessments, only one of which allows accommodations, is in some respects an attempt to equate test results for two different populations. Results of previous studies investigating the feasibility of linking large-scale assessments have shown that the linking functions can produce different results for different subpopulations (Linn and Kiplinger, 1995).

Accountability and Stakes

Changes in how tests are used inevitably lead to changes in how teachers and students react to them (Koretz, 1998). Indeed, one of the underlying rationales for test-based accountability is to spur changes in teaching and learning. The merits of using tests for such purposes are beyond the scope of this report. For our purposes, however, it is crucial to note that the difficulty of maintaining linkages between tests is exacerbated when consequences of test results for individuals or schools vary.

When test results have significant consequences, teachers may change what and how they teach to help students respond to the content and problems on the test (Shepard and Dougherty, 1991; National Research Council, 1999c), schools and districts may align curriculum more closely with test content, and test takers may have stronger motivation to do well (e.g., Koretz et al., 1991). Performance gains on tests used for accountability (high-stakes tests) will often not be reflected in scores on tests used for monitoring or other nonaccountability (low-stakes) purposes. The resulting differences in student performance could alter the relationship between linked tests over time (Shepard et al., 1996; Yen, 1996). Hence, any valid linkages created initially would have to be reestablished regularly.

The effects of test use on student and teacher behavior pose a special problem for linkage with NAEP. To protect its historical purpose as a monitor of educational progress, NAEP was designed expressly with safeguards to prevent it from becoming a high-stakes test. As a result, the motivation level of students who participate in NAEP may be low (O'Neil et al., 1992; Kiplinger and Linn, 1996), and they may not always exhibit peak performance. Linkages between a low-stakes instrument like NAEP and high-stakes state or commercial tests may not be sustained over time because teachers and students are likely to place greater emphasis on improving performance on the latter.

Reporting

One of the functions of state educational testing programs is to communicate, or report, results of student performance to parents, educators, policy makers, and the public. How results are aggregated and reported to these audiences, and the way these results are used, vary significantly among commercially published tests and state assessments, and these differences play a role in the ability to establish useful links between tests.

The results of student performance on a large-scale assessment may be reported in many ways. Results from tests intended to yield norm-referenced interpretations are often reported as grade equivalents, percentile ranks, stanines, or normal curve equivalents (see, e.g., Anastasi, 1982). These types of scores provide an indication of how the performance of students or groups of students who took the test compare with students in the same grade or of a similar age who were part of the norming sample. Criterion-referenced interpretations may be used to provide a status report or "snapshot" of what an individual student or all of the state's students know and are able to do in relation to the state's content standards or to other performance criterion. Individual student or group results earned on a criterion-referenced or standards-based assessment are most often reported in terms of "meeting the criterion or standard" or in terms of performance levels, which describe what students are expected to know and be able to do in order to be classified in each of the levels.

The level of data reported varies according to the purposes of the assessment and state requirements and specifications. Individual data may be reported for each test taker or aggregated and reported only at the school, district, or state level (Frechtling, 1993). Aggregated data may also be reported by various groupings, for example, by race, ethnicity, gender, school or district size, special education or nonspecial education program participation, accommodated or nonaccommodated assessment.

Comparing results earned on different types of measures and reported at different levels of aggregation is a challenge with serious implications for the ability to link tests to each other or to NAEP. Currently administered state and commercial achievement tests and NAEP vary significantly in terms of their content emphasis, types and difficulty of test questions, and the thought processes they require of students. In addition, these tests vary substantially in how and when they are administered, whether all students respond to the same sets of questions, how closely the tests are related to what is taught in school, how they are scored, and how the scores are reported and used (Roeber et al., 1998). Moreover, different test takers might use different cognitive processes on the same item. These factors contribute to the challenges faced by policy makers and others who seek to reconcile the dual goals of local control of educational decision making and national comparability and accountability.

5

Conclusions

The Committee on Equivalency and Linkage of Educational Tests was created to answer a relatively straightforward question: Is it feasible to establish an equivalency scale that would enable commercial and state tests to be linked to one another and to the National Assessment of Educational Progress (NAEP)? In this report we have attempted to answer this question by examining the fundamentals of tests and the nature of linking; reviewing the literature on linking, including previous attempts to link different tests; surveying the landscape of tests and testing programs in the United States; and looking at the unique characteristics and qualities of NAEP.

FACTORS THAT AFFECT THE VALIDITY OF LINKS

Test Content

A test is a sample of a much larger, more complex body of content, a domain. Test developers must make choices about the knowledge, skills, and topics from the domain they want to emphasize. The choices are numerous in a vast domain like reading or mathematics, where there are differing opinions about what should be taught, how it should be taught, and how it should be tested. Therefore, two state tests labeled "4th-grade reading" may cover very different parts of the domain. One test might ask students to read simple passages and answer questions about the facts and vocabulary of what they read, thereby testing simple recall and comprehension; another test might ask students to read multiple texts and make inferences that relate them, thereby testing analytic and interpretive reading skills.

Tests with different content may measure different aspects of performance and may produce different rankings or score patterns among test takers. For example, students who have trouble with algebra—or who have not yet studied it in their mathematics classes—may do poorly on a mathematics test that places heavy emphasis on algebra. But these same students might earn a high score on a test that emphasizes computation, estimation, and number concepts, such as prime numbers and least common multiples. When content differences are significant, scores from one test provide poor estimates of scores on another test: any calculated linkage between them would have little practical meaning and would be misleading for many uses.

Test Format

Tests are becoming more varied in their formats. In addition to multiple-choice questions, many state assessments now include more open-ended questions that require students to develop their own responses, and some include performance items that ask students to demonstrate knowledge by performing a complex task. Computer-based testing is another alternative format that has gained in popularity in recent years. The effects of format differences on linkages are not always predictable, and they are sometimes large (see, e.g., Shavelson et al., 1992).

Measurement Error

Every test is only a sample of a person's performance. If a test taker also took an equivalent, but not identical, test on a different day in a different place, her score is unlikely to be the same. That is, a test score always has some margin of error (which testing professionals call the standard error of measurement). Measurement error plays a role in the interpretation and use of scores on linked tests. If test A, with a large margin of error, is linked with test B, which is much more precise, the score of a person who took test A still has the margin of error of test A, even when reported in terms of the scale of test B. Students and test users can be misled by this difference in precision. A short test with unreliable (i.e., less precise) scores can seem to have more precision than it actually has if it is reported on the scale of the more reliable test.

Test Uses and Consequences

Variations in how tests are used, especially their consequences, can affect the stability of linkages over time. Many states are using or planning to use tests for high-stakes decisions, such as determining graduation for students, compensation for teachers, rating for schools or districts (National Research Council, 1999c). In contrast, other assessments, like NAEP, often have lower stakes for test takers, with no important consequences for individuals or others. When test stakes are low for them, students may have little incentive to take the test seriously; when they have reason to worry about the consequences of their scores, they are usually more motivated to try harder. When stakes are high, teachers are likely to alter instruction to try to produce higher scores, through such strategies as focusing on the specific knowledge, skills, and formats in that particular test. The strengths and weaknesses of these and other test-based accountability practices are controversial, and they are not the subject of this report. The important point for this report is that when a high-stakes test is linked with a low-stakes test, the relative difficulty of the two tests is likely to change (i.e., the high-stakes test will appear to become easier as the curriculum becomes aligned with it), and this can affect the stability of a linkage over time.

Evaluating Linkages

All of these factors—content emphases, difficulty, format, measurement error, and uses and consequences—point to the difficulty of establishing trustworthy links among different tests. But the extent to which any of these factors affects linkage can be determined only by a case-by-case evaluation of specific tests in a specific context. Developers of linkages should look carefully at the differences in content emphases, format, and intended uses of tests before deciding to link them. They should also set targets for the level of accuracy that will be required to support the intended uses of the linkage. Developers of linkages should also conduct empirical studies to determine the accuracy and stability of the linkage. In this report the committee suggests some criteria to be considered as part of this process. One noteworthy criterion is the similarity or dissimilarity of linkage functions developed using data from different subgroups (e.g., gender, ethnicity, race) of students.

Finally, since linkage relationships can change relatively quickly, especially in high-stakes situations, developers need to continue to monitor linkages regularly to make necessary adjustments to the linking function over time. The research literature is rife with examples of linkages that looked good at first but failed to hold up over time.

NAEP Achievement Levels

Even if two or more tests satisfy the appropriate criteria and prove to be amenable to linkage, linking any or all of them to NAEP poses unique challenges. This is particularly true when the goal of the linkage is to report individual student scores in terms of the NAEP achievement levels—basic, proficient, advanced—established and defined by the National Assessment Governing Board. Problems arise for several reasons.

First, NAEP is designed to estimate and report distributions of student scores by state, region, or the nation as a whole, *but it is not designed to report individual student scores.* It uses a matrix sampling technique in which each student answers a relatively small number of items from the total set then aggregates their scores in order to report group results. Such data are quite imprecise at the student level, and they are not well suited for use in standard procedures for linking individual scores (see, e.g., Beaton and Gonzalez, 1995). Most studies that have obtained links with the NAEP scale have prepared a test made from NAEP items, which was then given to individual students who had also taken the test being linked (see, e.g., Williams et al., 1995). Such NAEP stand-in tests must reflect the full content of the NAEP assessment and must also maintain the specific combination of item formats. They must also be administered in a way as nearly like the NAEP procedure as possible. Linking a test to a variant of NAEP that has a different mix of item formats, or a different balance of content, could produce a link whose validity is suspect (see, e.g., Linn et al., 1992).

Unique challenges arise in linking any other test with NAEP when the goal of the linkage is to report individual student scores in terms of the achievement levels. First, all test scores, including a NAEP score inferred from a linked test, have associated measurement error: even if a student took a different form of the same basic test, her score on that form might be somewhat higher or lower than the score she obtained on the form of the test she actually did take. The margin of error problem is not usually significant for students whose scores fall in the middle of an achievement category. It may be a problem, however, for students whose scores are near the border of two adjacent levels. Some of these students could easily deserve to be in an adjacent category. Every teacher knows that a high B and a low A could easily be reversed on another occasion. When NAEP estimates the proportion of students in each category, for its reports, such potential classification errors are accounted for. If the linked test is not a close match to NAEP, the classification differences can be substantial. This challenge might be addressed through a special administration of a longer version of NAEP, perhaps by testing students with many more items than they complete in a standard NAEP assessment.

Second, differences in formats or combinations in formats used in different tests are a special concern. Changing the proportion of multiple-choice items to constructed-response items could place a student in a different achievement level. Any special variant of NAEP designed for use in a linking study must maintain the mix of formats used in NAEP (as specified in the NAEP test specifications).

Over all, the committee urges caution in attempting to link achievement tests to NAEP and to report individual student scores on those tests in terms of the NAEP achievement levels.

CONCLUSIONS

Our findings, as summarized above, lead us to the following conclusions:

Comparing the full array of currently administered commercial and state achievement tests to one another, through the development of a single equivalency or linking scale, is not feasible.

Reporting individual student scores from the full array of state and commercial achievement tests on the NAEP scale and transforming individual scores on these various tests and assessments into the NAEP achievement levels are not feasible.

Under limited conditions it may be possible to calculate a linkage between two tests, but multiple factors affect the validity of inferences that may be drawn from the linked scores. These factors include the

context, format, and margin of error of the tests; the intended and actual uses of the tests; and the consequences attached to the results of the tests. When tests differ on any of these factors, some limited interpretations may be defensible, while others would not.

Links between most existing tests and NAEP, for the purpose of reporting individual students' scores on the NAEP scale and in terms of the NAEP achievement levels, will be problematic. Unless the test to be linked to the NAEP is very similar to NAEP in context, format, and uses, the resulting linkage could be unstable and potentially misleading. (The committee notes that it is theoretically possible to develop an expanded version of NAEP that could be used in conducting linkage experiments, which would make it possible to establish a basis for reporting achievement test scores in terms of the NAEP achievement levels. However, the few such efforts that have been made thus far have yielded limited and mixed results.)

The committee arrived at these conclusions notwithstanding the fact that we believe that the goal of bringing greater coherence to the reporting of student achievement data, without compromising the increasingly rich and innovative tapestry of tests in the United States today, is an understandable one. We respect both the judgments of states and districts that have produced the diverse array of tests and the desire for more information than current tests can provide. Furthermore, the committee was disposed, as are large segments of the measurement and educational policy communities, to seek a technological solution to the challenge of linking.

FUTURE RESEARCH

Despite our pessimism, we believe there are a number of areas where further research could prove fruitful and could help advance the idea of linkage of educational tests. First, we suggest research on the criteria for evaluating the quality of linkages. In its deliberations, the committee identified several such criteria, but we were unable to determine which were the most critical, and we cannot claim to have developed the exhaustive or definitive set of criteria. Additional study, for example on methods for assessing content congruence, could prove beneficial. The work of Kenney and Silver (1997) and of Bond and Jaeger (1993) represent important approaches to the problem. These researchers had to invent methods for establishing the extent to which test contents match; those methods need additional research and development, especially with respect to providing quantitative estimates of congruence that could be used in evaluating (predicting) the validity of proposed linkages.

Second, we suggest further research to determine the level of precision needed to make valid inferences about linked tests. We know that two tests that are built to different content frameworks, or to different test specifications, are looking at the test taker in two different ways. Each perspective may yield valid information, although not the same information. How important are the differences? Are they so minor that the differences can be overlooked? Are the biases sufficiently large to lead to misleading interpretations, or are they so small that they are inconsequential, although statistically detectable? And how can one determine what is "consequential"? What kind of guidelines do policy makers need in order to determine an acceptable level of error? In addressing these questions, the research community could make an important contribution to the policy debate by focusing on the marginal decrements in validity or precision of inferences that can be attributed to linkage, independent of the imprecision or invalidity attributable to the tests themselves. More research on methods of assessing the quality of linked assessment information would go a long way in making these important judgments

Finally, we urge further research on the reporting of linked assessment information. The committee found that one way of reporting a students' performance in terms of NAEP achievement levels is to state that, among 100 students who performed at the same level as the student, call her Sally, 10 are likely to be in the below basic category, 60 are likely to be basic; 28 are likely to be proficient; and 2 are likely to be in the highest, or advanced category.

While such information may be statistically valid, its utility is questionable. More research might point to ways in which reports from linking tests could provide information that is useful to students, parents, teachers, administrators, and policy makers.

References

Achieve, Inc.
  1998   About Achieve. Available electronically at http://www.achieve.org [March
          1].
Anastasi, A.
  1982   *Psychological Testing*, Fifth edition. New York: MacMillian Publishing Com-
          pany.
Beaton, A.E., and E.J. Gonzalez
  1993   Comparing the NAEP Trial State Assessment results with the IAEP interna-
          tional results. In *Setting Performance Standards for Student Achievement: Back-
          ground Studies*. Stanford, CA: National Academy of Education.
  1995   *The NAEP Primer*. Center for the Study of Testing, Evaluation, and Educa-
          tional Policy. Chestnut Hill, MA: Boston College.
Beaton, A.E., and R. Zwick
  1990   The Effect of Changes in the National Assessment: Disentangling the NAEP
          1985-1986 Reading Anomaly. Report No. 17-TR-21, Educational Testing
          Service, National Assessment of Educational Progress, Princeton, NJ.
Behuniak, P., and C. Tucker
  1992   The potential of criterion-referenced tests with projected norms. *Applied
          Measurement in Education* 5(4):337-353.
Bianchini, John C., et al.
  1974   Anchor Test Study. Final Report. Volume 1, Individual Norms and School
          Grade Norms, Grades 4, 5, and 6. Educational Testing Service, Berkeley,
          CA. ERIC microfiche collection, ED092602.
  1975   Investigation of the Appropriateness of the Anchor Test Study Equating Re-
          sults for Selected Subgroups. Final Report. Educational Testing Service,
          Princeton, NJ.

Bloxom, B., P.J. Pashley, W.A. Nicewander, and D. Yan
  1995   Linking to a large-scale assessment: An empirical evaluation. *Journal of Educational and Behavioral Statistics* 20 (Spring):1-26.
Bond, L., E. Roeber, and S. Connealy
  1998   *Trends in State Student Assessment Programs: Fall 1997.* Washington, DC: Council of Chief State School Officers.
Bond, L., and R.M. Jaeger
  1993   *Judged Congruence Between Various State Assessment Tests in Mathematics and the 1990 National Assessment of Educational Progress Item Pool for Grade-8 Mathematics.* Center for Educational Research and Evaluation. Greensboro NC: University of North Carolina.
Breland, H.M., et al.
  1994   Performance versus objective testing and gender: An exploratory study of an advanced placement history examination. *Journal of Educational Measurement* 31(4):275-293.
Campbell, J.R., P.L. Donahue, C.M. Reese, and G.W. Phillips
  1994   *NAEP 1994 Reading Report Card for the Nation and the States.* Office of Educational Research and Improvement, National Center for Educational Statistics. Washington, DC: U.S. Department of Education.
Cizek, G.J.
  1993   Reactions to National Academy of Education report, "Setting Performance Standards for Student Achievement." Unpublished letter written to the National Assessment Governing Board.
Cronbach, L.J.
  1984   *Essentials of Psychological Testing,* Fourth edition. New York: Harper & Row.
Education Week
  1998   *Quality Counts '98: The Urban Challenge: Public Education in the 50 States.* Washington, DC: Education Week.
Ercikan, K.
  1997   Linking statewide tests to the NAEP: Accuracy of combining test results across states. *Applied Measurement in Education* 10(2):145-159.
Feldt, L.S., and R.L. Brennan
  1989   Reliability. Pp. 105-146 *Educational Measurement,* Third edition. R.L. Linn, ed. New York: MacMillian Publishing Company.
Frechtling, J.A.
  1993   Administrative Uses of School Testing Programs. Pp. 475-483 in *Educational Measurement,* Third edition. R.L. Linn, ed. New York: MacMillian Publishing Company.
Glaser, R.
  1963   Instructional technology and the measurement of learning outcomes: Some questions. *American Psychologist* 18:519-521.
Gulliksen, H.O.
  1950   *Theory of Mental Tests.* New York: Wiley. (Reprinted 1995, Hillsdale, NJ: Erlbaum & Associates.)

Haertel, E.H.
1996   Test linking and comparability. In *Proceedings from the California Comparability Symposium, September 1997*. Los Angeles, CA: County Office of Education.

Herman, J.
1997   Large–Scale Assessment in Support of School Reform: Lessons in the Search for Alternative Measures. Center for the Study of Evaluation, National Center for Research on Evaluation. University of California, Los Angeles.

Hill, R.
1998   Using NAEP to Compare State Data—While It's Still Possible. Paper presented at the annual meeting of the National Council for Measurement in Education, San Diego, CA. Dover, NH: Advanced Systems, Inc.

Holland, P.W., and D.B. Rubin, eds.
1982   *Test Equating*. New York: Academic Press.

Jones, L.V.
1997   National Tests and Educational Reform: Are They Compatible? Policy Information Center, Educational Testing Service, Princeton, NJ.

Kane, M.
1993   Comments on the National Academy of Education Evaluation of the National Assessment Governing Board Levels. Unpublished letter.

Kenney, P., and E. Silver
1997   Content Analysis Project—State and NAEP Mathematics Assessment. Proposal Summary. Learning Research and Development Center, University of Pittsburgh.

Kentucky Department of Education
1995   *KIRIS Accountability Cycle I Technical Manual*. Frankfort: Kentucky Department of Education.

Kintsch, W.
1998   *Comprehension: A Paradigm for Cognition*. New York: Cambridge University Press.

Kiplinger, V.L., and R.L. Linn
1996   Raising the stakes of test administration: The impact on student performance on the National Assessment of Educational Progress. *Educational Assessment* 3(2):111-133.

Kolen, M.J., and R.L. Brennan
1995   *Test Equating: Methods and Practices*. New York: Springer-Verlag.

Koretz, D.
1998   Evidence Pertaining to the Validity of Score Gains on the Kentucky Instructional Results Information System (KIRIS). Paper presented at the symposium: Establishing Meaning: Validity Evidence for the Kentucky Instructional Results Information System (KIRIS), at the annual meeting of the National Council on Measurement in Education, April 16, San Diego, CA. RAND, Washington, DC.

Koretz, D., R.L. Linn, S. Dunbar, and L. Shepard
1991   The Effects of High-Stakes Testing on Achievement: Preliminary Findings About Generalization Across Tests. Paper presented at American Educational Research Association, April, Chicago, IL. RAND, Washington, DC.

Levine, R., A. Rathbun, R. Selden, and A. Davis
  1998   *NAEP's Constituents: What Do They Want?* Report of the NAEP Constituents' Survey and Focus Groups. Washington, DC: National Center for Education Statistics.

Linn, R L.
  1993   Linking results of distinct assessments. Applied Measurement in Education 6(1):83-102.

Linn, R.L., and V.L. Kiplinger
  1995   Linking statewide tests to the National Assessment of Educational Progress: Stability of Results. *Applied Measurement in Education* 8(2):135-156.

Linn, R.L., D.M. Koretz, E.L. Baker, and L. Burstein
  1991   *The Validity and Credibility of the Achievement Levels for the 1990 National Assessment of Educational Progress in Mathematics.* Los Angeles, CA: Center for Research on Evaluation Statistics.

Linn, R.L., L. Shepard, and E. Hartka
  1992   The relative standing of states in the 1990 trial state assessment: The influence of choice of content, statistics, and subpopulation breakdowns. In *Studies for the Evaluation of the National Assessment of Educational Progress Trial State Assessment.* Stanford, CA: National Academy of Education.

Lorch, R.F., and P. Van den Broek
  1997   Understanding reading comprehension: Current and future contributions of cognitive science. *Contemporary Educational Psychology* 22:213-247.

Lord, F.M., and M.R. Novick
  1968   *Statistical Theories of Mental Test Scores.* Reading, MA: Addison-Wesley.

Loret, P.G., A. Seder, J.C. Bianchini, and C.A. Vale
  1972   *A Description of the Anchor Test Study.* Princeton, NJ: Educational Testing Service.
  1973   The Anchor Test Study: Administration of the Study. Educational Testing Service, Princeton, NJ. Available ERIC microfiche collection, ED076672.

McDonnell, L.
  1994   *Policymakers' Views of Student Assessment.* CSE Technical Report 378. Los Angeles, CA: National Center for Research on Evaluation Standards, and Student Testing.
  1997   *The Politics of State Testing: Implementing New Student Assessments.* CSE Technical Report 424. Los Angeles, CA: National Center for Research on Evaluation, Standards, and Student Testing.

McLaughlin, D.
  1998   Study of the Linkages of 1996 NAEP and State Mathematics Assessments in Four States. Final Report. John C. Flanagan Research Center, Education Statistics Services Institute, American Institutes for Research. American Institutes for Research, Palo Alto, CA.

McLaughlin, M.W., L.A. Shepard, and J.A. O'Day
  1995   *Improving Education Through Standards-Based Reform.* Stanford, CA: National Academy of Education.

Mead, A.D., and F. Drasgow
  1993   Equivalence of Computerized and Paper-and-Pencil Cognitive Ability Tests: A Meta-Analysis. *Psychological Bulletin* 114:449-458.

Messick, S.
   1989   Validity. Pp. 13-103 in *Educational Measurement*, Third edition. R.L. Linn,
           ed. New York: MacMillan Publishing Company.
Mislevy, R.J.
   1992   *Linking Educational Assessments: Concepts, Issues, Methods, and Prospects.*
           Princeton, NJ: Educational Testing Service.
Mislevy, R.J., A.E. Beaton, B. Kaplan, and K.M. Sheehan
   1992   Estimating population characteristics from sparse matrix sample of item re-
           sponses. *Journal of Educational Measurement* 29:131-154.
Mosteller, F.C.
   1995   The Tennessee study of class size in the early school grades. *The Future of
           Children: Critical Issues For Children and Youths* 5(2):113-127.
National Center for Education Statistics
   1998   *Linking the National Assessment of Educational Progress and the Third Interna-
           tional Mathematics and Science Study: Eighth Grade Results.* Eugene Johnson
           and Adriane Siegendorf, eds. NCES 98-500. Washington, DC: U.S. De-
           partment of Education.
National Council of Teachers of English
   1996   *Standards for the English Language Arts: A Joint Project of the National
           Council of Teachers of English and the International Reading Association.*
           Urbana, IL: National Council of Teachers of English.
National Council of Teachers of Mathematics
   1989   *Curriculum and Evaluation Standards for School Mathematics.* Reston, VA: Na-
           tional Council of Teachers of Mathematics.
National Research Council
   1996   *Evaluation of "Redesigning the National Assessment of Educational Progress."*
           Committee on the Evaluation of National and State Assessments of Educa-
           tional Progress, Board on Testing and Assessment, National Research Coun-
           cil. Washington, DC: National Academy Press.
   1998   *Preventing Reading Difficulties in Young Children.* Catherine E. Snow, M. Susan
           Burns, and Peg Griffin, eds. Committee on Preventing Reading Difficulties
           in Young Children, Commission on Behavioral and Social Sciences and Edu-
           cation. Washington, DC: National Academy Press.
   1999a   *Evaluation of the Voluntary National Tests: Phase 1.* L.L. Wise, R.M. Hauser,
           K.J. Mitchell, and M.J. Feuer. Board on Testing and Assessment, National
           Research Council. Washington, DC: National Academy Press.
   1999b   *Grading the Nation's Report Card: Evaluating NAEP and Transforming the As-
           sessment of Educational Progress.* J. Pellegrino, L. Jones, and K. Mitchell, eds.
           Committee on the Evaluation of National and State Assessments of Educa-
           tional Progress, Board on Testing and Assessment. Washington, DC: Na-
           tional Academy Press.
   1999c   *High Stakes: Testing for Tracking, Promotion, and Graduation.* Jay P. Heubert
           and Robert M. Hauser, eds. Committee on Appropriate Test Use, Board on
           Testing and Assessment, National Research Council. Washington, DC: Na-
           tional Academy Press.

O'Neil, H.F., B. Sugrue, J. Abedi, E. Baker, and S. Golen
  1992   *Final Report of Experimental Studies on Motivation and NAEP Test Performance.* Los Angeles, CA: Center for Research on Evaluation, Standards, and Student Testing.

Pashley, P.J., and G.W. Phillips
  1993   *Toward World-Class Standards: A Research Study Linking International and National Assessments.* Center for Educational Progress. Princeton, NJ: Educational Testing Service.

Peterson, N.S., M.J. Kolen, and H.D. Hoover
  1993   Scaling, norming, and equating. Pp. 221-262 in *Educational Measurement*, Third edition. R.L. Linn, ed. New York: MacMillan Publishing Company.

Poyla, G.
  1980   On solving mathematical problems in high school. In *Problem Solving in School Mathematics: 1980 Yearbook*, S. Krulik, ed. Reston, VA: National Council of Teachers of Mathematics.

Pressley, M. and P. Afflerbach
  1995   *Verbal Protocols of Reading: The Nature of Constructively Responsive Reading.* Hillsdale, NJ: Lawrence Erlbaum Associates.

Roeber, E., L. Bond, and S. Connealy
  1998   *Annual Survey of State Student Assessment Programs. Fall 1997.* Washington, DC: Council of Chief State School Officers.

Shavelson, R.J., G.P. Baxter, and J. Pine
  1992   Performance assessments: Political rhetoric and measurement reality. *Educational Researcher* 21(4):22-27.

Shepard, L.A., R.G. Glaser, and R. Linn
  1993   *Setting Performance Standards for Student Achievement: A Report of the National Academy of Education of the NAEP Trial State Assessment: An Evaluation of the 1992 Achievement Levels.* Stanford, CA: National Academy of Education.

Shepard, L.A., R.J. Flexer, E.H. Hiebert, and S.F. Marion
  1996   Effects of introducing classroom performance assessments on student learning. *Educational Measurement Issues and Practices* 15(3):7-18.

Shepard, L.A., and K.C. Dougherty
  1991   Effects of High Stakes Testing on Instruction. Paper presented at the meeting of the American Educational Research Association/National Council on Measurement in Education, Chicago, IL. University of Colorado, Boulder.

Stufflebeam, D.M., R.M. Jaeger, and M. Scriven
  1991   *National Assessment Governing Board's Inaugural 1990-91 Effort to Set Achievement Levels on the National Assessment of Educational Progress.* Washington, DC: National Assessment Governing Board.

U.S. Congress, Office of Technology Assessment
  1992   *Testing in American Schools: Asking the Right Questions.* OTA-SET-519, February 1992. Washington, DC: U.S. Government Printing Office.

U.S. Department of Education, National Center for Education Statistics
  1997   *The NAEP Guide.* J. Calderone, L.M. King, and N. Harkay, eds. National Center for Education Statistics. NCES 97-990. Washington, DC: U.S. Department of Education.

U.S. General Accounting Office
  1993   *Educational Achievement Standards: NAGB's Approach Yields Misleading Inter-pretations.* GAO/PEMD-93-12. Washington, DC: U.S. Government Printing Office.

Virginia Department of Education
  1997   The Virgina State Assessment Program: *Transition From the Iowa Tests of Basic Skills and the Tests of Academic Proficiency to the Stanford 9.* Virginia Department of Education.

Waltman, K.K.
  1997   Using performance standards to link statewide achievement results to NAEP. *Journal of Educational Measurement* 34(2):101-121.

Wester, Anita
  1995   The importance of the item format with respect to gender differences in test performance: A study of open-format items in the DTM Test. *Scandinavian Journal of Educational Research* 39(4):335-346.

Williams, V., K. Billeaud, L. Davis, D. Thissen, and E. Sanford
  1995   *Projecting to the NAEP Scale: Results from the North Carolina End-of-Grade Testing Program.* Technical Report #34. Chapel Hill, NC: National Institute of Statistical Sciences, University of North Carolina, Chapel Hill.

Wu, G., M. Royal, and D. McLaughlin
  1997   Development of a SASS 1993-94 School-Level Student Achievement Subfile: Using State Assessments and State NAEP. Feasibility Study. Education Statistics Services Institute, American Institutes for Research, Washington, DC.

Yen, W.
  1996   Linking Tests for AB 265. In *Proceedings from the California Comparability Symposium, September 1997.* Los Angeles, CA: County Office of Education.
  1998   Linking Assessment to NAEP and Providing Individual Student Scores. Paper presented to the Committee on Equivalency and Linkage of Educational Tests, March. CTB-McGraw Hill, Monterey, CA.

Yen, W., and S. Ferrara
  1997   The Maryland School Performance Assessment Performance Program: Performance assessment with psychometric quality suitable for high stakes usage. *Journal of Educational and Psychological Measurement* 57(1):60-84.

Glossary

This glossary provides definitions of terms as used in this report. Note that technical usage may differ from common usage. For many of the terms, multiple definitions can be found in the literature. Words set in *italics* are defined elsewhere in the Glossary.

Achievement levels/proficiency levels Descriptions of student or adult competency in a particular subject area, usually defined as ordered categories on a continuum, often labeled from "basic" to "advanced," that constitute broad ranges for classifying performance. NAEP defines three achievement levels for each subject and grade being assessed: basic, proficient, and advanced. NAGB describes the knowledge and skills demonstrated by students at or above each of these three levels of achievement, and provides exemplars of performance for each. In addition, NAGB also reports the percentage of students who are in four categories ranges of achievement as defined by the three levels. These achievement categories are generally labeled below basic, basic, proficient, or advanced. NAGB does not provide a description for the below basic category.

ACT American College Testing Assessment. A set of tests designed to predict college performance from current achievement, used in college admissions produced by the American College Testing Program.

Alternate forms   Two or more versions of a test that are considered interchangeable, in that they measure the same constructs, are intended for the same purposes, and are administered using the same directions. Alternate forms is a generic term used to refer to any of three categories. Parallel forms have equal raw score means, equal standard deviations, and equal correlations with other measures for any given population. Equivalent forms do not have the statistical similarity of parallel forms, but the dissimilarities in raw score statistics are compensated for in the conversions to derived scores or in form-specific norm tables. Comparable forms are highly similar in content, but the degree of statistical similarity has not been demonstrated; also called equivalent forms.

Anchor test   A common set of items administered with each of two or more different tests for the purpose of equating the scores of these tests.

Assessment   Any systematic method of obtaining evidence from tests and collateral sources used to draw inferences about characteristics of people, objects, or programs for a specific purpose; often used interchangeably with test.

ASVAB   Armed Services Vocational Aptitude Battery. A set of 10 tests used for entrance into U.S. military service.

Bias   In a test, a systematic error in a test score. In a linkage, a systematic difference in linked values for different subgroups of test takers. Bias usually favors one group of test takers over another.

Calibration   The process of setting a test score scale, including the mean, standard deviation, and possibly the shape of the score distribution, so that scores on the scale have the same relative meaning as scores on a related score scale.

CCSSO   Council of Chief State School Officers. A nationwide, non-profit organization of public officials who head departments of elementary and secondary education. Through standing and special committees, CCSSO responds to a broad range of education concerns.

Classical test theory   The view that an individual's observed score on a test is the sum of a true score component for the test taker, plus an independent measurement error component. A few simple premises about these components lead to important relationships among validity, reliability, and other test score statistics.

Comparable forms See *alternate forms*.

Composite score A score that combines several scores by a specified formula.

Confidence interval An interval between two values on a score scale within which, with specified probability, a score or parameter of interest lies.

Content congruence The extent of similarity of content in two or more tests.

Content domain The set of behaviors, knowledge, skills, abilities, attitudes or other characteristics measured by a test, represented in a detailed specification, and often organized into categories by which items are classified.

Content standard A statement of a broad goal describing expectations for students in a subject matter at a particular grade range or at the completion of a level of schooling.

Constructed-response item An exercise for which examinees must create their own responses or products rather than choose a response from an enumerated set.

Correlation A measure of the degree of relationship between two paired sets of values on two variables. In this report, it usually refers to the relationship of scores on two tests, taken by a set of students. The index ranges from 1.0, signifying perfect agreement, through 0.0, representing no agreement at all, to −1.0, representing perfect negative agreement, with high scores on one variable associated with low scores on the other.

Criterion-referenced test A test that allows users to estimate the amount of a specified content domain that an individual has learned. Domains may be based on sets of instructional objectives, for example. Also called domain-referenced tests.

Cutscore   A specified point on a score scale, such that scores at or above that point are interpreted differently from scores below that point. Sometimes there is only one cut score, dividing the range of possible scores into "passing" and "failing" or "mastery" and "nonmastery" regions. Sometimes two or more cut-scores may be used to define three or more score categories, as in establishing performance standards. See *performance standard.*

Distribution   The number, or the percentage, of cases having each possible data value on a scale of data values. (In testing, data values are usually test scores.) Distributions are often reported in terms of grouped ranges of data values. A distribution can be characterized by its mean and standard deviation.

Distribution matching   *Equipercentile equating*, but with possibly different populations.

Domain-referenced test   See *criterion-referenced test.*

Domain   The full array of a particular subject matter being addressed by an assessment.

Domain sampling   The process of selecting test items to represent a specified universe of performance.

Effect size   A measure of the practical effect of a statistical difference, usually a difference of the means of two distributions. The mean difference between two distributions, or an equivalent difference, is expressed in units of the standard deviation of the dominant distribution or of some average of the two standard deviations. For example, if two distributions had means of 50 and 54, and both had standard deviations of 10, the effect size of their mean difference would be 4/10, or 0.4. The effect size is sometimes called the standardized mean difference. In other contexts, other ways are sometimes used to express the practical size of an observed statistical difference.

Equating The process of statistical adjustments by which the scores on two or more alternate forms are placed on a common scale. The process assumes that the test forms have been constructed to the same explicit content and statistical specifications and administered under identical procedures.

Equipercentile A type of nonlinear equating in which the entire score distribution of one test is adjusted to match the entire score distribution of the other for a given population. See *distribution matching*. Scores at the same percentile on two different test forms are made equivalent.

Equivalency scale A term used to refer to a score scale that has been linked to the scale of another measure.

Equivalent forms See *alternate forms*.

Error of measurement The amount of variation in a measured value, such as a score, due to unknown, random factors. In testing, measurement error is viewed as the difference between an observed score and a corresponding theoretical true score or proficiency. See *standard error of measurement*.

ETS Educational Testing Service. A not-for-profit organization that produces tests for many testing programs, including the College Entrance Examination Board's Scholastic Assessment Test (SAT).

Form In testing, a particular test in a set of tests, all of which have the same test specifications, and are mutually equated.

Framework The detailed description of the test domain in the way that it will be represented by a test.

High-stakes test A test whose results has important, direct consequences for examinees, programs, or institutions tested.

ITBS Iowa Tests of Basic Skills. A series of commercial achievement tests in various school subjects, authored at the University of Iowa and published by Riverside Publishing Company, Inc.

Item   A generic term used to refer to a question or an exercise on a test or assessment. The test taker must respond to the item in some way. Since many test questions have the grammatical form of a statement, the neutral term item is preferred.

Item format   The form in which a question is posed on a test and the form in which the response is to be made. They include, among others, selected-response (multiple-choice), and constructed-response formats, which may be either short-answer, or extended-response items.

Item pool   The aggregate of items from which a test's items are selected during test development or the total set of items from which a particular test is selected for test taker during adaptive testing.

Item response theory (IRT)   A theory of test performance that emphasizes the relationship between mean item score (P) and level (4) of the ability or trait measured by the item. In the case of an item scored 0 (incorrect response) or 1 (correct response), the mean item score equals the proportion of correct responses. In most applications, the mathematical function relating P to 4 is assumed to be a logistic function that closely resembles the cumulative normal distribution.

Linkage   The result of placing two or more tests on the same scale so that scores can be used interchangeably. Linking methods include *equating, calibration, statistical moderation,* and *social moderation.*

KIRIS   Kentucky Instructional Results Information System   An assessment developed by the Kentucky Department of Education, which primarily uses performance tasks.

Linear equating   A form of equating in which the scores on one test are transformed linearly to be equal to the mean and standard deviation of another test. Sometimes both sets of test scores are transformed so that each has a common mean and standard deviation.

Low-stakes test   A test whose results has only minor or indirect consequences for the examinees, programs, or institutions tested.

LSAT Law School Admissions Test. A large-scale test administered to applicants for admission to law schools.

Matrix sampling A measurement format in which a large set of test items is organized into a number of relatively short item sets, each of which is randomly assigned to a subsample of test takers, thereby avoiding the need to administer all items to all examinees.

Mean The numerical average of a set of data values, such as test scores.

Measurement error variance That portion of the observed score variance attributable to one or more sources of measurement error; the square of the standard *error of measurement*.

Metric The units in which the values on a scale are expressed.

Moderation See *statistical moderation, social moderation*. Used without a modifier, the term usually means statistical moderation.

MSPAP Maryland State Performance Assessment Project. A state-produced assessment in several school subjects, containing only extended performance tasks. Some matrix sampling is used in its administration.

NAEP National Assessment of Educational Progress. An assessment given periodically to a representative sample of U.S. students in 4th, 8th, and 12th grades in reading, mathematics, social studies, and science, and in other subjects on an occasional basis. Since 1990, a separate state-by-state assessment has also been conducted.

NAGB National Assessment Governing Board, responsible for policy governing the NAEP.

Normal distribution A particular form of data distribution, with a definite mathematical form. A normal distribution is symmetric in shape, with relatively many values concentrated near the mean, and relatively few that depart greatly from the mean. A normal distribution is specified by its mean and standard deviation. About 68 percent of the values are within 1 standard deviation of the mean, about 96 percent are within 2 standard deviations of the mean, and nearly all values are within 3 standard deviations of the mean. Many distributions of test scores are approximately normal in shape. The term "normal" is used to connote customary, or related to the norm, not ideal.

Normalized standard score A derived test score in which a numerical transformation has been chosen so that the score distribution closely approximates a normal distribution for some specific population.

Norm-referenced test A test on which scores are interpreted on the basis of a comparison of a test taker's performance to the performance of other people in a specified reference population.

Norms Statistics or tabular data that summarize the distribution of test performance for one or more specified groups, such as test takers of various ages or grades. Norms are usually designed to represent some larger population, such as all test takers in the country. The group of examinees represented by the norms is referred to as the *reference population*.

Parallel forms See *alternate forms*.

Percentile The score on a test below which a given percentage of test takers' scores fall.

Percentile rank The percentage of scores in a specified distribution that fall below the point at which a given score lies.

Performance assessments Product- and behavior-based measurements based on settings designed to emulate real-life contexts or conditions in which specific knowledge or skills are actually applied.

Performance standard An objective definition of a certain level of performance in some *domain* in terms of a *cutscore* or a range of scores on the score scale of a test measuring proficiency in that domain. Also, sometimes, a statement or description of a set of operational tasks exemplifying a level of performance associated with a more general *content standard*; the statement may be used to guide judgments about the location of a *cutscore* on a score scale.

Pilot test   A test administered to a representative sample of test takers solely for the purpose of determining the properties of the test.

Precision of measurement   A general term that refers to the reliability of a measure, or its sensitivity to *error of measurement*.

Projection   A method of linking based on the regression of scores from one test (test B) onto the scores of another test (test A). The projected score is the average B score for all persons with a given A score. See *regression*. The projection of test B to test A is different from the projection of test A to test B.

Random error   An unsystematic error; a quantity (often assessed indirectly) that appears to have no relationship to any other variable.

Raw score   The unadjusted score on a test, often determined by counting the number of correct answers, but more generally a sum or other combination of item scores.

Reference population   The population of test takers represented by test norms. The sample on which the test norms are based is intended to permit accurate estimation of the test score distribution for the reference population. The reference population may be defined in terms of the test taker's age, grade, clinical status at time of testing, or other characteristics.

Regression   A statistical procedure for estimating the value associated with an entity on one variable, called the dependent variable, from the values of that entity on one or more other variables, called independent variables. The term without modification usually refers to linear least-squares regression, in which the values for an entity on the independent variables are combined linearly to form an estimate of the dependent variable. The linear combination is developed using values for a sample of entities on all the variables and finding the linear combination that minimizes the average squared discrepancy between the estimated value and the actual value for the sample.

Regression coefficient   A multiplier of an independent variable in a linear equation that relates a dependent variable to a set of independent variables. Can also be understood as the marginal effect of a change in an independent variable or the value of the dependent variable. The coefficient is said to be standardized or unstandardized as the variable it multiplies has been scaled to a standard deviation of 1.0 or has some other standard deviation, respectively.

Relative score interpretations   The meaning of a score for an individual, or the average score for a definable group, derived from the rank of the score or average within one or more reference distributions of scores.

Reliability   The degree to which the scores are consistent over repeated applications of a measurement procedure and hence are dependable, and repeatable; the degree to which scores are free of errors of measurement. Reliability is usually expressed by a unit-free index that either is, or resembles, a product-moment correlation. In classical test theory, the term represents the ratio of true score variance to observed score variance for a particular examinee population. The conditions under which the coefficient is estimated may involve variation in test forms, measurement occasions, raters, or scorers, and may entail multiple examinee products or performances. These and other variations in conditions give rise to qualifying adjectives, such as alternate-forms reliability, internal-consistency reliability, test-retest reliability, etc.

SAT   (1) Scholastic Assessment Test, the College Entrance Examination Board's test designed to predict college performance. The test battery contains a verbal section, and a mathematics section, as well as specialized subject tests. It is produced by ETS. (2) Stanford Achievement Test, a set of achievement tests used for student assessment in some states, produced by Harcourt Brace Educational Measurement.

Scale score   A score on a test that is expressed on some defined scale of measurement. See *scaling*.

SCASS   A project of the Council of Chief State School Officers, the State Collaborative on Assessment and Student Standards is designed to help states develop student standards and assessments working together with other states with similar needs.

Scaling   The process of creating a scale score. Scaling may enhance test score interpretation by placing scores from different tests or test forms onto a common scale or by producing scale scores designed to support criterion-referenced or norm-referenced score interpretations.

Score   Any specific number resulting from the assessment of an individual; a generic term applied for convenience to such diverse measures as test scores, production counts, absence records, course grades, ratings, and so forth.

Scoring rubric   The principles, rules, and standards used in scoring an examinee performance, product, or constructed response to a test item. Scoring rubrics vary in the degree of judgment entailed, in the number of distinct score levels defined, in the latitude given scorers for assigning intermediate or fractional score values, and in other ways.

Selected-response item   Test item for which test taker selects response from provided choices; also known as multiple-choice item.

Social moderation   An adjustment in the values of test scores to adjust for known social factors affecting test scores for a group of test takers.

Standard error of measurement   The standard deviation of the distribution of errors of measurement that is associated with the test scores for a specified group of test takers.

Standard score   A type of derived score such that the distribution of these scores for a specified population has convenient, known values for the *mean* and *standard deviation*.

Standard deviation   An index of the degree to which a set of data values is concentrated about its mean. Sometimes referred to as "spread." The standard deviation measures the variability in a distribution of quantities. Distributions with relatively small standard deviations are relatively concentrated; larger standard deviations signify greater variability. In common distributions, like the mathematically defined "normal distribution," roughly 67 percent of the quantities are within (plus or minus) 1 standard deviation from the mean; about 95 percent are within (plus or minus) 2 standard deviations; nearly all are within (plus or minus) 3 standard deviations. See also *distribution, effect size, normal distribution, variance.*

Standardization   In test administration, maintaining a constant testing environment and conducting the test according to detailed rules and specifications so that testing conditions are the same for all test takers. In statistical analysis, transforming a variable so that its standard deviation is 1.0 for some specified population or sample.

Statistical moderation   An adjustment of the score scale of one test, usually by transforming the scores so that their mean and standard deviation are equal to the mean and standard deviation of another distribution of test scores. It is statistically equivalent to *linear equating*, the simplest form of linking. See also *social moderation*.

Systematic error   A score component (often observed indirectly), not related to the test performance, that appears to be related to some salient variable or subgrouping of cases in an analysis. See *bias*.

Test   A set of items given under prescribed and standardized conditions for the purpose of measuring the knowledge, skill, or ability of a person. The person's responses to the items yield a score, which is a numerical evaluation of the person's performance on the test.

Test development   The process through which a test is planned, constructed, evaluated and modified, including consideration of the content, format, administration, scoring, item properties, *scaling*, and technical quality for its intended purpose.

Test specifications   A *framework* that specifies the proportion of items that assess each content and process or skill area; the format of items, responses, and scoring protocols and procedures; and the desired psychometric properties of the items and test, such as the distribution of item difficulty and discrimination indices.

Test user   The person(s) or agency responsible for the choice and administration of a test, the interpretation of test scores produced in a given context, and any decisions or actions that are based, in part, on test scores.

TIMSS   Third International Mathematics and Science Study. An assessment given in 1995 to samples of students in a large number of countries.

Unbiased The obverse of biased. See *bias*.

Validation The process of investigation by which the validity of the proposed interpretation of test scores is evaluated.

Validity When applied to a test, an overall evaluation of the degree to which accumulated evidence and theory support specific interpretations of test scores. When applied to a linkage of two or more tests, the extent to which the scores can from one test can be interpreted in the same way as the scores from others.

Variance A measure of the spread of data values, such as test scores; the square of the *standard deviation*. The variance is the mean of the squared deviations of the data values from their mean.

VNT Voluntary National Tests. Proposed by President Clinton in 1997, achievement tests that states could choose to give to assess performance of 4th-grade students in reading, and 8th-grade students in mathematics. Intended as a nationally sponsored test yielding individual student scores compared to national (and international) benchmarks.

Biographical Sketches

Paul W. Holland (*Chair*), is a professor in the Graduate School of Education and the Department of Statistics at the University of California, Berkeley. He is participating in the Berkeley Evaluation and Assessment Research Project, where he and others are working to develop new assessment techniques and evaluation methodologies for practical application in schools. He serves on a design and technical advisory committee for the National Assessment of Educational Progress (NAEP). Dr. Holland earned a Ph.D. degree in statistics from Stanford University.

Lisa D. Alston is a senior project assistant with the Board on Testing and Assessment. Previously, she held a variety of positions at the National Research Council, including technical auditing assistant with the Office of Internal Audit and as an administrative assistant for the Office of the Chief Financial Officer. She has extensive experience in the areas of accounting and internal audit. Ms. Alston is completing work for a B.S. degree in business administration and children, family, and public policy from Trinity College, Washington, D.C.

Meryl W. Bertenthal is a senior research associate with the Board on Testing and Assessment. She is on leave from the Charlottesville, Virginia, Public Schools, where she serves as the secondary-level curriculum and instructional coordinator and the division director of testing. Her interest areas include the appropriate use of educational tests, curriculum development, gifted education, and the development of guidance and counseling services for middle and high school students. Ms. Bertenthal earned an M.A.Ed. degree from Clark University and completed a specialist program in school counseling at the University of Virginia.

Robert C. Calfee is a professor and the dean of the School of Education at the University of California, Riverside. He was formerly a professor of education and psychology in the School of Education at Stanford University. His research focuses on the effect of schooling on the intellectual potential of individuals and groups; the nature of human thought processes; the influence of language and literacy in the development of problem-solving and communication skills; the effects of testing and other educational indicators; and ability grouping, teacher assessment, and the psychology of reading. Dr. Calfee earned a Ph.D. degree in cognitive psychology from the University of California, Los Angeles.

Michael J. Feuer is director of the Board on Testing and Assessment. His past positions include senior analyst and project director, U.S. Office of Technology Assessment, where he directed studies on testing and assessment, vocational education, and educational technology, and assistant professor, Department of Management and Organizational Sciences, at Drexel University. His major areas of interest include human resources, education, and public policy. He has published numerous articles in scholarly journals as well as in the popular press. Dr. Feuer received a B.A. degree from Queens College, City University of New York, and M.A. and Ph.D. degrees from the University of Pennsylvania.

Bert F. Green is a professor of psychology, emeritus, at the Johns Hopkins University. He is a member of a national committee that is revising the Standards for Educational and Psychological Testing. He serves on the Maryland State Department of Education's psychometric council for the Maryland School Performance Assessment Program. His research concerns psychometric methods for computer-based adaptive testing, as well as performance assessment and health assessment. Dr. Green earned a Ph.D. degree in psychology from Princeton University.

John T. Guthrie is a professor in the Department of Human Development at the University of Maryland, College Park, and is the former codirector of the National Reading Research Center. His current research focuses on how classroom context facilitates the acquisition of reading as a multifaceted set of strategic motivational and conceptual processes. He serves on the National Assessment of Educational Progress (NAEP) Standing Committee on Reading and Writing, the original NAEP reading framework design committee, and other national committees. He has published secondary analyses of NAEP data relating reading achievement to student background and classroom instructional characteristics. Dr. Guthrie earned a Ph.D. degree in educational psychology from the University of Illinois.

F. Cadelle Hemphill is a senior research associate with the Board on Testing and Assessment. Previously, she worked as a senior program associate at the American Institutes for Research, Education Statistics Services Institute, where she managed the Advisory Council on Education Statistics activity. As a senior project associate at the Council of Chief State School Officers, she codirected the annual large-scale assessment conference and managed the Education Information Advisory Committee. Her research interests include educational assessment as it relates to education policy and reform. She holds an A.B. degree in public policy studies from Duke University.

Viola C. Horek is administrative associate of the Board on Testing and Assessment. Before joining the board, she worked at the Board on Agriculture and the Committee on Education Finance of the National Research Council. Previously, she worked for the city of Stuttgart, Germany, as an urban planner and for the U.S. Department of Defense in Germany. Ms. Horek received an M.A. degree in architecture and urban planning from the University of Stuttgart.

Richard M. Jaeger is the NationsBank professor of educational research methodology and the director of the Center for Educational Research and Evaluation at the University of North Carolina, Greensboro. He is past president of the National Council on Measurement in Education. His research is concerned with educational measurement and applied statistics. He is a member of the National Assessment of Educational Progress (NAEP) Validity Studies Panel. Dr. Jaeger earned an M.S. degree in mathematical statistics and a Ph.D. in educational research methodology from Stanford University.

Patricia Ann Kenney is a research associate at the University of Pittsburgh's Learning Research and Development Center (LRDC). She is codirector of two projects related to the National Assessment of Education Progress (NAEP) in mathematics, one of which involves the development of a process through which the content of state-level mathematics assessments and NAEP can be compared. Previous research includes work related to the verification of the content and curricular validity of the NAEP Trial State Assessment in Mathematics and issues pertaining to the learning of college-level mathematics. Dr. Kenney earned a Ph.D. degree in mathematics education, with specializations in mathematical statistics and educational measurement, from the University of Texas at Austin.

Vonda L. Kiplinger is an assessment specialist for the Colorado Department of Education Student Assessment Program. Her early research focused on linking statewide tests to the National Assessment of Educational Progress (NAEP). Currently, she is investigating the feasibility of linking large-scale state assessments to the NAEP and TIMSS (Third International Mathematics and Science Study) and is examining the Colorado NAEP-TIMSS linkage anomaly. Dr. Kiplinger earned a Ph.D. degree in research and evaluation methodology from the University of Colorado School of Education.

Nancy Kober is a freelance writer, editor, and consultant specializing in education and science. She has written and edited dozens of publications for government agencies, nonprofit organizations, private foundations, and trade publishers. She was a contributor to and editor of a national study of educational testing produced by the U.S. Office of Technology Assessment. She also she teaches workshops in writing skills to federal executives and managers. Previously, Ms. Kober served as a legislative specialist for the U.S. House of Representatives, Subcommittee on Elementary, Secondary, and Vocational Education.

Daniel M. Koretz is a senior social scientist at the RAND Institute on Education and Training in Washington, D.C., and a professor of educational research, measurement, and evaluation at Boston College. A primary focus of his work is educational assessment, particularly as it relates to educational policy and reform. His research interests include the diverse effects of assessment programs on schooling and learning, the quality of information yielded by both conventional and innovative assessments, and evaluations of indicators of elementary and secondary mathematics and science education. Dr. Koretz received a Ph.D. degree in developmental psychology from Cornell University.

Frederick C. Mosteller is professor emeritus of statistics at Harvard University and serves as the director of the Technology Assessment Program at the Harvard School of Public Health. He is a member of the National Academy of Sciences and the Institute of Medicine. His research interests focus on theoretical statistics and its applications to social science, medicine, public policy, and industry. Dr. Mosteller received a Ph.D. degree in mathematics from Princeton University.

Peter J. Pashley is the director of psychometrics at the Law School Admission Council (LSAC) in Newtown, Pennsylvania. His current research efforts are centered on psychometric methods, particularly item response theory, linking proficiency scales and assessments, computer-based testing, and psychometric models for item response time data. He has participated in two large-scale linking studies: the first linked the International Assessment of Education Progress (IAEP) to the National Assessment of Educational Progress (NAEP), and the second linked the Armed Services Vocational Aptitude Battery (ASVAB) to NAEP. Dr. Pashley received a Ph.D. degree in quantitative psychology from McGill University.

Doris Redfield is an educational consultant specializing in issues related to assessment, standards, evaluation, and related educational policy. She formerly served as director of assessment for the Commonwealth of Virginia Department of Education. Her current work is focused on the development of technical guidelines for large-scale assessments; standards setting, particularly as it relates to Title I legislation; professional development pertaining to new national, federal, state, and local student assessment initiatives; and issues surrounding the assessment of special needs and limited English proficient students. Dr. Redfield received a Ph.D. degree in educational psychology, research, measurement, and evaluation from the University of Arizona.

William F. Tate is associate professor of mathematics education in the Department of Curriculum and Instruction at the University of Wisconsin, Madison. He is a senior researcher at the Wisconsin Center for Education Research. His current area of research focuses on opportunity-to-learn issues in mathematics education. Other research interests include mathematics education reform, developing models for mathematical technology, and mathematics assessment. Dr. Tate received a Ph.D. degree in mathematics education from the University of Maryland.

David Thissen is a professor of psychology, director of the graduate program in quantitative psychology, and the acting director of the L.L. Thurstone Psychometric Laboratory at the University of North Carolina, Chapel Hill. His research interests include psychometrics and item response theory, models for human growth and development, and graphics and statistics in psychological contexts. He is currently investigating issues related to linking North Carolina educational assessment test results to the National Assessment of Educational Progress (NAEP) scale. Dr. Thissen received a Ph.D. degree in behavioral sciences from the University of Chicago.

Ewart A.C. Thomas is a professor of psychology at Stanford University, having previously served a term as dean of the university's School of Humanities and Sciences. His research interests include the development and application of mathematical and statistical models to many areas of psychology and social sciences, with particular focus on signal detection, information processing, motivation, assessment of group differences, parent-infant interaction, categorization, and inter-rater reliability. He is also pursuing research in theoretical population biology, the dynamics of language variation, law and social sciences, and economic planning in developing countries. Dr. Thomas received a Ph.D. degree in statistics from the University of Cambridge, England.

Lauress L. Wise is president of the Human Resources Research Organization (HumRRO). His research interests focus on issues related to testing and test use policy. He recently served on the National Academy of Education's Panel for the Evaluation of the National Assessment of Educational Progress (NAEP) Trial State Assessment and is currently serving on the National Research Council's Committee on the Evaluation of NAEP. Prior to joining HumRRO, he directed research and development of the Armed Services Vocational Aptitude Battery (ASVAB) for the U.S. Department of Defense. In that capacity, he oversaw a study investigating the feasibility of linking ASVAB and NAEP mathematics scores. Dr. Wise received a Ph.D. degree in mathematical psychology from the University of California, Berkeley.